MARCO ⊕ POLO

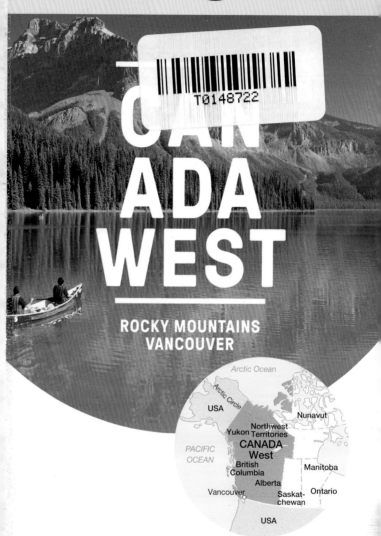

CANADA WEST

ROCKY MOUNTAINS
VANCOUVER

Arctic Ocean

Arctic Circle

USA

Yukon

Northwest
Territories

Nunavut

PACIFIC
OCEAN

CANADA
West

British
Columbia

Alberta

Manitoba

Vancouver

Saskat-
chewan

Ontario

USA

www.marco-polo.com

FREE!

THE TOURING APP

shows you the way...
including routes and offline maps!

GET MORE OUT OF YOUR MARCO POLO GUIDE

SYMBOLS

INSIDER TIP Insider Tip

★ Highlight

●●●● Best of ...

↘⃫ Scenic view

♦ Responsible travel: for
fair trade and ecology
aspects

(*) Telephone numbers
that are not toll-free

**PRICE CATEGORIES
HOTELS**

Expensive over C$240
Moderate C$130–240
Budget under C$130

Rates are per double room
without breakfast. Single
rooms are rarely cheaper

**PRICE CATEGORIES
RESTAURANTS**

Expensive over C$35
Moderate C$25–35
Budget under C$25

The prices are for a main meal
in the evening, including
taxes. At lunchtime it is about
40–50 per cent cheaper

CONTENTS

DID YOU KNOW?
Timeline → p. 14
Innovative Canadians → p. 25
Local specialities → p. 28
Virtual view of fixed-rope
climbing routes → p. 70
Dining like a trapper? → p. 77
Caution: bear ahead! → p. 80
For bookworms & film
buffs → p. 132

MAPS IN THE GUIDEBOOK
(138 A1) Page number and
coordinates refer to the road
atlas
Coordinates are also given
for places that are not
marked on the road atlas
(U A1) Coordinates for the
map of Vancouver on the
inside back cover
Map of Calgary → p. 86

(ᗡ A–B 2–3) Refers to the
removable pull-out map
(ᗡ a–b 2–3) Refers to the
additional map on the pull-
out map

INSIDE FRONT COVER:
The best Highlights

INSIDE BACK COVER:
Map of Vancouver

The best
MARCO POLO
Insider Tips

Our top 15 Insider Tips

INSIDER TIP **On a bear hunt – with a camera**

With a little luck you will be able to see some of the resident black bears up close from the boat in the bays around *Tofino*. In the summer the bear mothers here teach their cubs how to crack mussels → **p. 44**

INSIDER TIP **Starfish ahoy!**

Seemingly weightless floating jellyfish, colourful sea anemones, giant octopus, starfish, wolf eels and many other marine animals live in the *Shaw Centre for the Salish Sea* (photo above) north of Victoria – but only for a while, then they are returned to the sea → **p. 49**

INSIDER TIP **Picture-perfect town**

The historic trading post of *Fort Langley* on the Fraser River has often been the backdrop for Hollywood movies – with a little luck you might cross paths with a star who is filming a movie there → **p. 39**

INSIDER TIP **Visit the culinary world of Asia**

Strange spices, durian fruit, live crabs and duck feet: the *T & T Supermarket* on the edge of Chinatown in Vancouver offers all the gourmet treasures of Asia → **p. 35**

INSIDER TIP **A river full of salmon**

In early October the *Adams River*, north-east of Kamloops, swarms with hundreds of thousands of bright red salmon → **p. 56**

INSIDER TIP **Log cabins on the lake**

Thick beams, red roofs and breathtaking vistas: the *Clearwater Lake Lodge* off Hwy. 20 meets all the requirements for a wilderness adventure → **p. 53**

INSIDER TIP **Hot springs in the wilderness**

Pure relaxation after a long walk: soak sore muscles in the *Nakusp Hot Springs* pools, wonderfully secluded in the woods → **p. 61**

BEST OF ...

FOR FREE

● *Salmon viewing in Vancouver*
Instead of going to an aquarium, you can see wild salmon up close and for free at the *Capilano Salmon Hatchery* in the summer. Watch the fish fight against the flow through large underwater observation windows → p. 34

● *Gold rush town*
Historic *Dawson City* could almost be a museum village, but the authentic gold rush town established in 1898 is alive and kicking and offers wonderful photo opportunities and plenty of pioneer flair (photo) without any entrance fee → p. 95

● *Sunny mountains, dizzying heights*
National parks charge admission but provincial parks in Alberta, such as *Kananaskis Country,* are free. The Rocky Mountains here are just as beautiful as in Banff – but much sunnier, because it is the eastern flank of the mountains → p. 77

● *The sound of the mountains*
Enjoy jazz, classical music, dance and even operas – for free or only little money – throughout the summer at the prestigious *Banff Centre*. All in front of the magnificent mountain scenery of Banff National Park → p. 89

● *Enjoyment of art for free*
'Art for all' is the motto of the *Vancouver Art Gallery* every Tuesday evening, when admission is free. Those who want to, can leave a donation. Worth seeing: Emily Carr's impressionistic and expansive paintings of the rugged west coast → p. 38

● *Cliff hiking*
Landscaped and paved trails are few and far between on the west coast – and they usually cost money such as in the Pacific Rim National Park. The *Wild Pacific Trail* right next door in Ucluelet is free and truly stunning. Start with the Lighthouse Loop section! → p. 44

●●●●● Dots in guidebook refer to 'Best of...' tips

ONLY IN WESTERN CANADA
Unique experiences

● *Celebrate with lumberjacks*
It doesn't get more Canadian than the *Salmon Festival* in Campbell River on Vancouver Island where salmon and lumberjacks are celebrated – with axe throwing and bowsaw competitions → p. 127

● *Driving to the Arctic Ocean*
The trip on Canada's northernmost road takes two days: the 700 km/435 mi *Dempster Highway* runs through the wilderness from Dawson City across the Arctic Circle and to the polar sea → p. 97

● *Orca watching*
It is a strict rule that no one is allowed to get closer than 100 m/328 ft from the whales. But the inquisitive creatures often come closer to the boats and you may experience this on a whale watching tour in Victoria with *Eagle Wing Tours* → p. 48

● *Smoked salmon in Vancouver*
At the Granville Island *Public Market* in Vancouver you can sample the culinary treasures of Canada's west coast: raspberries, goat's cheese, oysters, halibut – and the best smoked salmon in the world → p. 35

● *Trapper for a day*
How about spending the night as a fur trapper? Deep in the wilderness of British Columbia the wooden stockades and beaver pelts of the *Fort St James National Historic Site* take you back to the era of the fur trader → p. 64

● *Cycling around Stanley Park*
On a sunny afternoon, there is no better outing in Vancouver than the more than 10 km/6.2 mi long *Stanley Park Drive*. The route winds its way along the coast with great views of the city, the mountains, the fjords and small beaches → p. 36

● *Lake views in the Rocky Mountains*
The view from *Bow Summit Pass* – 2000 m/6562 ft and sometimes windy – over Peyto Lake is quite stunning. The strikingly turquoise glacial lake is one of the most impressive sights in the Rockies (photo) → p. 69

ONLY IN

BEST OF ...

RAIN

● *Outlet shopping in Calgary*
Shopping is cheap (and you will stay dry) in *Crossiron Mills* in Calgary, the largest indoor discount mall in Canada. Some 200 shops offer everything from stilettos to Stetsons → **p. 87**

● *Dinosaurs in Drumheller*
Alberta's badlands experience intense thunderstorms with pouring rain, and if you get caught in one then take refuge in Drumheller's *Royal Tyrrell Museum* (photo). The bonus: when it rains, the fossil beds are laid bare – perhaps you will discover a new type of dinosaur → **p. 89**

● *Underwater in the Vancouver Aquarium*
Spend a rainy day in the large, well designed *Vancouver Aquarium*, where animals like sea otters and fur seals can be observed → **p. 36**

● *A rain forest in the rain*
Rain forests flourish on the west coast of Vancouver Island, for example in the *Pacific Rim National Park*. Naturally it rains here often. Whales and bears are not disturbed by the rain – and hopefully you won't either will you be → **p. 44**

● *Take a ferry ride up the coast*
Dark pine forests, blue fjords, leaping orca: on a trip through the *Inside Passage* you can sit high and dry and let the mystical, misty fjord world pass you by → **p. 46**

● *Drown your sorrows in the Ranchman's Saloon*
Your bad weather blues will disappear with beer, tasty ribs and country songs in the *Ranchman's Saloon* in Calgary. When it rains you have an even greater chance of meeting some real cowboys – they knock off work earlier then → **p. 87**

RELAX AND CHILL OUT
Take it easy and spoil yourself

● *View the Rockies from a boat*

Why should you hike if you can enjoy an even more beautiful view from the water? The half-day *Waterton Shoreline Cruise* (in a historic little boat) shows the southern Rockies in Canada from their best side – and you can even make a whistlestop visit over the border into the United States → p. 79

● *A spa on a ranch*

After the ride enjoy a relaxing massage – the *Echo Valley Ranch* in the BC heartland offers a real Thai spa with soothing treatments, massages, herbal baths and yoga classes. Worth seeing: the original Thai bathhouse → p. 57

● *Drinking wine in the Okanagan Valley*

The sunny slopes along the lakes of Okanagan Valley have some of Canada's best vineyards. If you are a lover of wine or simply enjoy the idea of tasting something new, do take the time and indulge in some wine tasting on the terrace of the *Mission Hill Winery* at Kelowna → p. 58

● *Relax in hot springs*

Nothing could be better on a wet, cold day than to relax in some hot mineral water. The *Radium Hot Springs* (photo) are ideal for this, but there are also other places in the Rockies where you can quickly ease your aching muscles → p. 73

● *Dive into a crystal world*

A cold sauna? Yes, that is right, at an eye-watering −120 °C/−184 °F (very briefly) the skin and immune system are stimulated. The spa of the *Sparkling Hill Resort* in Vernon also boasts a unique crystal décor that corporates 3.5 million Swarovski crystals → p. 60

● *Into the wilderness on the Yukon*

Another way to relax is to canoe on the Yukon River from Whitehorse to Dawson City. Slowly paddle and drift through the wilderness. Equipment and rental canoes are available at *Kanoe People* in Whitehorse → p. 99

INTRODUCTION

DISCOVER
WESTERN CANADA!

In an ever more crowded world, Canada possesses two significant advantages: lots of space and plenty of wild nature. This is the ideal place for outdoor enthusiasts to live the dream, to watch a family of bears on the shores of a fjord, enjoy the silence of the mighty Yukon River, to camp with cowboys in the vastness of the prairies or to go rafting through wild river rapids.

Somehow people believe that they know Canada. It lies on the same latitude as central Europe, and the climate is not much different from that of Europe, the mountains somewhat resemble the Alps, the coasts resemble those of Norway. And yet, Western Canada is completely different – huge, epic, impressive, lonely. It lacks people, the noisy motorways and urban sprawl. Instead there is an unending and vast expanse of nature, and almost every hike up to a mountain summit is rewarded with a panoramic view of a landscape without roads or houses. Here the breathtaking landscape is still unspoilt and pristine.

First of all, you will have to get used to *Canada's dimensions*. A trip to the next shop that could be situated 50 km/31.1 mi away is barely worth mentioning. The West of

Photo: Moraine Lake

The skyline of cosmopolitan Calgary, mirrored in the facade of the new Bow Towers

Canada, the provinces of Alberta and British Columbia, the Yukon and the Northwest Territories, covers more than *1 million mi²*. You could fit France and Germany into the province of British Columbia alone, which only has 4.6 million inhabitants.

For a first trip to Canada the western part, with its varied landscapes, is the ideal destination. On the *fjord-dotted Pacific coast*, the glaciercrowned Coast Mountains rise up, with their ancient and mysterious rain forests, from the dark waters, the home of whales and king salmon. Behind the mountains lie sunny plateaus rich in forests and lakes – interspersed with mountain ranges – that extend out as far as the Rocky Mountains. *The Rocky Mountains* have the most beautiful national parks in the country, Banff and

Fjord coasts and mountains crowned with glaciers

Around 35,000 BC
Paleoamericans migrate across the Bering Strait to North America

1535/1536
Frenchman Jacques Cartier discovers the St Lawrence River and uses the name Canada

1670
Royal charter by King Charles II establishes the Hudson's Bay Company, granting a monopoly over the fur trade and incorporating the land in the drainage basin of Hudson Bay

1763
New France becomes a British colony; fur traders open up the west

Jasper, connected by the Icefields Parkway, a spectacular scenic road. Even further eastwards, *beyond the Rockies*, is the ranch country of Alberta, where dinosaurs roamed more than 60 million years ago, as evidenced by the *rich*

> **The second-largest oil reserves in the world**

fossil finds along the Red Deer River. Today, large herds of cattle graze there – in a bizarre coexistence with the oil pumps that extract Alberta's black gold. With the huge deposits of tar sands around Fort McMurray in northern Alberta, Canada has the *second largest oil reserves in the world*, after Saudi Arabia. There and on the *large wheat fields* in the southern part of the region, it is clear that the economy largely depends on agriculture and the abundant raw materials. In recent decades, demand for raw materials has created a boom in the western provinces of Canada, but the low oil price and the growing resistance of the population against pipelines is now slowing down the energy sector.

In the far north there are the sparsely green mountain ranges and valleys of the *Yukon and the Northwest Territories*. About 100 years ago this was where the *greatest gold rush in history* took place – and since forgotten. The *climatic contrasts* here are as varied as the landscapes: damp, mild marine climate prevails on the Pacific coast, while in the interior of Canada there is a continental climate with hot summers and bitterly cold winters. High in the Arctic North, summer barely lasts two months while in the South – on the same latitude as the French wine region of Champagne – the Okanagan Valley in British Columbia is temperate enough

1778
The British explorer James Cook explores the Pacific coast

1792/93
Alexander Mackenzie crosses the continent to the Pacific Ocean

1821
North West Company of Montreal and Hudson's Bay Company merge, their combined territory make the company the largest private landowner in the world

1867
The birth of Canada: in the British North America Act the colonies of Ontario, Québec, Nova Scotia and New Brunswick are declared the *Dominion of Canada*

for vineyards and peach orchards to thrive. But even the extreme heat of summer, in the prairies of Alberta, and the polar cold of the Arctic winter, are tempered by the low humidity.

Only about *35 million people* live in Canada, only around 9 million in the entire western region. There is a lot of space left and the vast area is ideal for camping, fishing, hiking, canoeing and horseback riding. But it need not only be all about the wilderness experience. You also need to see the towns and cities. *Vancouver – surrounded by the sea –* is considered one of the most beautiful cities on the North American continent. The few cities are also the only enclaves of modern civilisation in Western Canada. Only the south, the region along the border with the United States, is made accessible by highways and settlements. *About 80 per cent of the population* lives in the fertile valley of the Fraser River, in the temperate valleys around Kelowna and Kamloops and in Alberta's two metropolises. However, the *mountain and Arctic areas are almost deserted*.

> ## Hot summers and bitterly cold winters

The western region of Canada is the youngest part of the country – both historically and geographically. *Only 30 million years ago* the Rocky Mountains were thrust upward from the sedimentary layers of the ancient seas. The continental drift of the Pacific Plate against the North American mainland forced up a series of mountain ranges: this area is known as the Pacific Cordillera and is the youngest of Canada's geographic regions. Roughly 30,000 years ago the *ancestors of the Native Americans* moved across the *Bering Strait* and then through Western Canada and from there settled throughout the rest of the continent. Their descendants are still strongly represented in the region today. They live in small villages in their old tribal areas, and are managing their rights and identity with growing self-confidence; this is especially evident along the western coast where their *totem poles and plank houses* can still be admired.

Much later, some 200 years ago, *the first white explorers*, the British Captain Cook and Captain Vancouver, sailed along the west coast and began to trade fur with the Native Americans. It was only at the beginning of the 19th century that the

1871
British Columbia joins the *Dominion of Canada*

1885
Completion of the Canada Pacific Railway line. Banff, the first Canadian National Park, is established

1898
Gold rush at Klondike. First oil find in Alberta

1931
Canada is a sovereign state in the *Commonwealth*

1942
Construction of the Alaska Highway

1962
Completion of the Trans-Canada Highway

first real settlers arrived: farmers from the Ukraine, from England, Germany and Scandinavia. And just 120 years ago the first cities arose, and the *first railway* from Montréal steamed westwards.

The distinctive black and white orcas are often seen around Vancouver Island

Economically the West Canadians have remained true to the land: *mining, ranching, fisheries, wheat* and recently even *wine*, are the main industries in the southern provinces. *Forestry* is the mainstay in the relatively unexplored north, where cutting down dead trees infected by the bark beetle currently provides plenty of work. Still, there are huge, totally unspoilt and uninhabited landscapes, in part under *permanent conservation*, such as the nearly 4000 mi² of Tweedsmuir Provincial Park.

Western Canada is a paradise for wildlife enthusiasts with endless opportunities for adventure. But why test your limits? A comfortable tour in a camper can give you a *sense of freedom and space* too.

A paradise for wildlife enthusiasts

Canada is not really about ticking off attractions. Take the time to enjoy long mountain hikes, to explore wild beaches, to relax at a campfire barbecue or to just breathe in the clean air of this unspoilt country.

1965
Canada adopts the maple leaf national flag

1990s
A wave of immigration from Hong Kong brings 70,000 Chinese to Vancouver

2010
Olympic Winter Games in Vancouver

2015
Declining oil prices and protests against new pipelines have weakened the raw material sector

2017
Huge fires destroy an area of more than 10,000 km² / 3861 mi² forest in British Columbia

WHAT'S HOT

1 Eye-catching

Art Not only the works of art are worth seeing, but so are the exhibition rooms, such as the *Van Dop Gallery (421 Richmond St. | New Westminster) (photo)*, integrated into the rooms of a private house. The *Truck Gallery (www.truck.ca)* in Calgary also displays its works in a camper-van throughout the city. For the *Fuse Night* the *Vancouver Art Gallery (750 Hornby St.)* regularly transforms itself into a party location with very whacky performances. The *Hotel Arts (119 12th Ave. SW | Calgary)* is the perfect choice for music lovers.

Downhill

2

Sport A Kitewing *(www.kitewing.com)* attached to skis, snowboard or skates lets you fly over the snow-fields. When Dirtsurfing the name is program: you surf on mountain bikes over rubble and snow. *Sooke Cycle (2075 Anna Marie Rd. | Sooke)* is one of the hot spots on Vancouver Island. Splitboard is popular for tours into the hinterland *(www.splitboard.com)*, a snowboard divided vertically into two parts. With the board you can go uphill like on skis and – once clipped together – whiz back down on a snowboard. The Kootenays are a popular area for it.

3 Delicious

Ice cream Chocolate or strawberry would be too simple. The latest flavours include salted caramel, rosemary-lavender and toasted coconut. The scoops are also enormous. Young people are experimenting everywhere at the moment in new ice cream shops, e.g. in Vancouver at *Rain or Shine (1926 W 4th Ave.)*, *Earnest Icecream (1829 Quebec St.) (photo)* and *Village Ice Cream in Calgary (431 10 Ave. SE)*.

Calgary rocks

Music Canada's fourth largest city takes first place over Toronto and Vancouver in the matter of music. It is home to a thriving music scene and the hometown of *The Dudes (www. wearethedudes.com)*. Live music is not played in impersonal halls but in pubs with stages, such as in *Ship & Anchor (534 17th Ave SW)*, *Drum and Monkey (1201 1st St. SW)* and *Broken City (613 11th Ave SW)*. The concert venues become crowded in June when the *Sled Island Music and Arts Festival (www.sledisland.com)* attracts all sorts of outlandish and flamboyant musicians to the city.

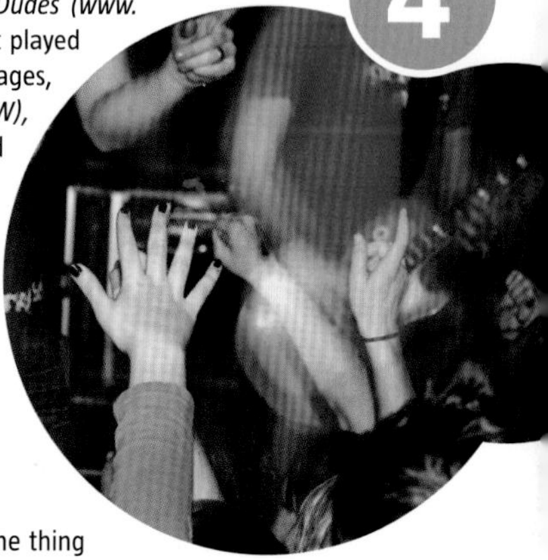

4

Two in one

Shopping Why only concentrate on one thing at a time? Multitasking is all the rage in Vancouver's super chic boutique *Secret Location (1 Water St.)* which not only sells fashion and quirky lifestyle objects, but also amazing gourmet food at flashily styled dining tables. Further east in Vancouver's industrial district, you can drink both freshly brewed beer and local freshly pressed wine in *Settlement Building (55 Dunlevy Ave. | vancouverurbanwinery.com)*. Variety is also the catchword at Calgary's *Tubby Dog (1022 17th Ave. SW)*: concerts and art displays on the walls accompanied by snacks and video games from the 1980s. In Edmonton's 🌏 *Carbon Environmental Boutique (112543 102 Ave. NW)* you can salve your environmental conscience and also buy particularly environmentally friendly baby clothing. And *AntiSocial (2337 Main St.) (photo)* in Vancouver's trendy neighbourhood in the Main Street looks almost like an art gallery, but actually sells fashionable skater clothing.

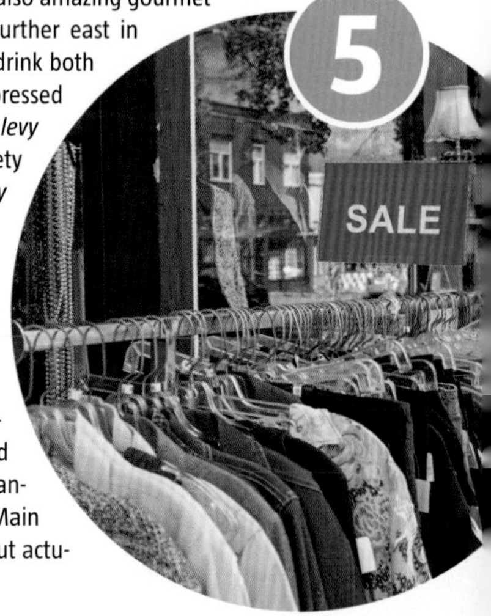

5

SALE

IN A NUTSHELL

FLORA & FAUNA

Most of Western Canada lies in the area of the boreal forest, which stretches in a broad band across the continent. These forests are the habitat of bears, moose, several deer, lynxes, porcupines and beavers, and more recently the bark beetle – possibly a result of global warming – which is wreaking havoc in the interior of British Columbia.

To the north, the forests of taiga and tundra extend into the Yukon and the Northwest Territories. Only caribou, mountain hares and musk ox can live off the sparse lichens and mosses in this region. However, in the summer the large freshwater areas nourish countless waterfowl.

The south and east of Alberta form part of the large North American prairie, orig-inally a grass savannah, but due to its fer-tile soil the area is now mostly ploughed and covered by massive crop fields. What was once the home to millions of bison is today the breadbasket of Canada – there are bison in only a few protected areas. Al-pine flora, with many wild flowers, flour-ishes in the Rocky Mountains, providing nourishment to mountain goats and sheep. On the western slopes of the Coast Mountains and on Vancouver Island there are lush rain forests full of tall Douglas firs, Sitka spruces, red cedars and lush ferns.

THE HUNT FOR THE PUCK

During the winter, Saturday evening is always 'Hockey Night in Canada'. The entire nation sits in front of the TV or

The Queen and the puck rule Canada – astonishing and fundamental facts about the maple leaf country

in sports bars, cheers on the teams of the *National Hockey League (NHL)* and laughs at the sharp suits worn by the legendary commentator Don Cherry. The US teams are also followed intensively as numerous players in the American teams come from Canada.

The seamen who travelled with the English explorer John Franklin during the 19th century supposedly played hockey on the ice, thus establishing today's most popular sport in Canada. When the home teams play off for the famous Stanley Cup, then the whole country is in hockey fever. The best teams of the West are *Vancouver Canucks, Calgary Flames* and *Edmonton Oilers*.

Tip: tickets for NHL games (Oct–April) are expensive and not always easy to purchase. You can however buy tickets on entry at the mostly equally exciting games in the regional and college leagues.

FIRST NATIONS

The descendants of the original inhabitants of Canada are not Indians or

Eskimos – the politically correct term is *First Nations*. With this term, Canadians recognise that the 617 tribes in the country were living there long before white people arrived. The ancestors of the Native Americans probably came across the Bering Strait to North America 15,000–35,000 years ago. Over the course of millennia they developed into independent cultural groups, with the semi-nomadic hunter tribes living in the north. The Plains tribes (today they are called Alberta) followed the massive herds of buffalo, while the Kwakiutl and Haida on the west coast had such a rich food supply that they had enough leisure time to become skilled woodcarvers. The ancestors of today's Inuit crossed the Canadian Arctic from Alaska about 1000 years ago. Today, there are around 700,000 Native Americans and 50,000 Inuit of those 'First Nations' in the country. Their rights as the original inhabitants of the continent were acknowledged with a section in the 1982 Constitution Act. This, and their strengthening self-confidence of indigenous people, led to numerous movements for land restitution and self-governance. The Inuit achieved the most spectacular success with this – in 1999 they received their own territory separate from the Northwest Territories, known as *Nunavut* (our land), which they govern and manage themselves.

P ROTECTED FOR ALL ETERNITY

The forerunner of present-day Banff National Park was founded in 1885 'for the benefit, advantage and enjoyment of the people of Canada'. It was the first in what is now a long list of parks, where the most beautiful and most pristine regions of the vast countryside are protected. The ecological aspects of the park system, mandated by the Canadian ministry of the environment, were considered to be groundbreaking. The country's 47 national parks today cover a total of approximately 116,000 mi^2; a further dozen parks are planned.

Approximately 30 million people visit the parks annually, and visitor must abide by park rules: no animals may be fed, no branch broken. Picking a bouquet of wild flowers can be an expensive experience: you may be fined up to C\$500. Hunting is naturally also prohibited. However, you may fish in the streams and lakes – with a fishing license of course. For additional information see: *www.parkscanada.ca*.

G OD SAVE THE QUEEN

A surprising and yet true fact: Queen Elizabeth II is Canada's head of state as the nation is a parliamentary democracy within the British Commonwealth. The Queen does however not have any power over the nation, but performs occasional ceremonial tasks and either she or the princes pay a visit to the country around every ten years.

The federal capital is Ottawa, but Canada's ten provinces have extensive autonomy in matters of education, cultural policy, health care and use of natural resources. Only the three sparsely populated territories in the north are financed and governed largely from Ottawa.

G RAND CINEMA

If you look very closely, you can recognise the landscapes of the Rockies or Vancouver in particular films. Numerous Hollywood movies are actually filmed in West Canada which offers the double advantage of fantastic scenery and low production costs. Vancouver is top of the list of filming locations. 'Deadpool 2' for example was recently shot here.

Stars such as Ben Stiller, Lucy Hale and Liam Neeson are frequently spotted here. The Rockies provide a great backdrop for Westerns: Marilyn Monroe was filmed here in 'River of No Return' and both 'Brokeback Mountain' and the classic film 'Little Big Man' were shot in the foothills of the mountains.

ENVIRONMENTAL PROTECTION

Sustainability is the key word of the Canadian organic movement. Despite the fact that the conservative government in the most environmentally friendly city in the world by 2020 is building bike paths and a commuter railway system. While Western Canada is the birthplace of powerful environmental organisations – such as the *David Suzuki Foundation*, *Living Oceans Society* and *Greenpeace* – the country is still one of the world's largest squanderers. No wonder, because the Canadians have always had an abundant supply of mineral resources, energy and water, but they are now rethinking their ways. Learn more about environmental issues in Canada: *thegreenpages.ca*.

Traditional meeting of chiefs: powwow festival of the Blackfoot tribe

Ottawa opted out of the Kyoto Protocol for climate protection, many Canadians see themselves as being environmentally conscious. Rubbish is separated and recycled, nature parks are created and environmental organisations are actively supported. Vancouver even plans to become

JUSTIN, THE CHARMER

The new Prime Minister of Canada is young and sexy. He portrays himself as being in touch with the populace, lists boxing as his hobby and was a high school teacher prior to his election. Justin Trudeau is the new political star of

The Mounties normally only wear their red jackets at ceremonies and when on horseback

Canada. His political talent is in his blood as the son of the former Prime Minister Pierre Trudeau who enjoyed great popularity during the 1970s and his hippy wife Margaret. Since his election in 2015, he has distinguished himself politically, brought women and minority individuals into the cabinet, retained a distance to Donald Trump and set up an airlift to bring Syrian refugees to Canada. He is also known for viral videos and photos as can be seen on YouTube.

MOUNTIES

Dressed in red, the *Royal Canadian Mounted Police* are probably Canada's most famous and recognised symbol. In their parade uniform the *Mounties* perform at official events. However, they are much more than just a colourful accessory; today the highly trained federal police are responsible for all rural regions and jurisdictions in Canada that cannot afford their own police – and there are many in the sparsely populated west. Founded in 1873, the RCMP force is today about 15,000 strong. For decades, the forts of the Mounties were also the only outposts of civilisation in the then rather wild west. The lawmen patrolled the Arctic with dog sleds, on horseback and by canoe, and went into the most isolated gold mining camps. And even today you can experience the Mounties up close and personal – as armed guards on the highways who will fine you if you exceed the speed limit!

POP STARS? OH YES!

When Peter Fonda made the famous road trip movie 'Easy Rider' the bikers cruised along on the open road to the legendary song 'Born to be Wild'. The soundtrack was by the band Steppenwolf and the members mostly came from Toronto. A typical case in point, as Canada never had its own independent pop music: Hollywood and the American music scene were too dominant, which is why many Canadian artists such as Leonard Cohen, Neil Young and Joni Mitchell all moved down to the States. The Canadian musicians that are currently famous include Bryan Adams, Céline Dion, Alanis Morissette, Avril Lavigne, Justin Bieber and country singer Shania Twain.

WOODEN OSTENTATION

Adorned with elaborate, carved masks, mythical animals and totem poles stand in front of government buildings and museums. Kitsch plastic replicas decorate the souvenir shops. Totem poles are the most recognisable symbol of Native American culture. Originally, this highly developed wood carving art was only part of the culture of the Northwest Coast Native Americans – the area between Vancouver Island and Southeast Alaska. Totem poles were not religious icons but symbols of prestige for a clan or a chief in demonstrating power and wealth. For decades the 'pagan carvings' were banned by the state and missionaries, but this ancient art form is undergoing a revival. You can see the most beautiful totem poles in the museums of Vancouver and Victoria. Or drive to the Native American villages up the west coast, where many original totem poles have been preserved, such as in Alert Bay, Quadra Island and Hazelton.

GOLD

After the publication of Jack London's novels almost everyone knows the story of the Klondike gold rush. Actually the search for the precious metal played a very special role in Canadian history, because the discovery of gold opened up the whole western region. Around 1860 the gold rush in the Cariboo Mountains attracted thousands of miners. 30 years later the call of 'Gold in the Yukon!' and 100,000 gold diggers toiled laboriously through ice and snow in the Coast Mountains to reach the promised land in time for spring. In just three years gold worth 100 million dollars was found, and Dawson City became the largest city west of Winnipeg with 30,000 inhabitants.

Gold is still being mined to this day – in Klondike, in Yellowknife and in the hard granite rock of the Canadian Shield in Eastern Canada – some four million ounces annually, of which a large part goes to the *Maple Leaf Dollar*, one of the best selling gold coins in the world.

INNOVATIVE CANADIANS

Telephone, matches, and the zipper – did you know that they all come from Canada? And the Canadians have invented a whole lot more, such as the snowmobile and the combine harvester. In 1879 the enormous size of Western Canada led the railway engineer Sanford Fleming to divide the earth into 24 time zones. Canada has also contributed with medical innovations: in 1929 Frederick Banting and Charles Best developed the diabetes drug insulin, and the engineer John Hopps developed the first pacemaker in 1951. Today Canadian researchers are at the forefront of AIDS and genetic research.

FOOD & DRINK

There is no Canadian national dish – the immigrant groups from all continents were too different, the country too large. Instead, it is the diversity of specialities that is the charm of the multicultural culinary delights of Western Canada.

In all the major cities, you will be able to enjoy *excellent Chinese, Indian and Italian restaurants*. There is also sushi; the fresh fish from the Pacific is of the highest quality, making sushi a very popular choice. Aside from *fresh salmon* (in many varieties) there is, of course, also Canada's famous *grilled steak*, often served with baked potatoes and corn on the cob.

Of course you will also be confronted with the usual fast foods, the monot-

ony of hamburgers and grilled chicken. There are fast food restaurants serving breakfast and lunch everywhere in Canada. But if you put a little effort in and look beyond the flashing neon signs you will find smaller venues offering home cooked meals – in the small fish restaurants on Vancouver Island, in rustic lodges in the wilderness or in ethnic restaurants in the cities – and then you will be pleasantly surprised.

In Alberta, you have to try a steak – either in a restaurant or barbecued on your own campfire. The cattle roam wild on huge ranches and the meat is unsurpassable, and the *portions are designed for hungry lumberjacks*. West of the Rocky Mountains seafood is the main culinary attraction, deliciously

Photo: Ceasar Salad

Canada's culinary charms lie in the diversity of local ingredients and the recipes brought here by the immigrants

fresh on Vancouver Island and along the Sunshine Coast north of Vancouver. Poached or grilled salmon (the sockeye salmon is best) with fresh vegetables from Fraser Valley and a crisp white wine from sunny Okanagan Valley is among the finest Canada has to offer.

In the style of the new *California cuisine* that emerged in the 1970s in San Francisco and Los Angeles, Vancouver and Victoria have developed a similar **west coast style**. The methods of preparation and the spices used come from all over the world – from France as well as from Asia. The produce, however, is ecologically sound i.e. locally grown. Vegetables from the Fraser Valley, peaches, apples and grapes from the Okanagan Valley, crab, halibut and salmon straight from the Pacific.

The talented young chefs understand how best to make the different flavours harmonize and how best to bring out the different tastes. And sometimes, they also include traditional cooking methods such as when the salmon is

LOCAL SPECIALITIES

bannock – Scottish flatbread baked in a pan (adapted by the Native Americans as fry bread)

beavertail – fried pastry sprinkled with cinnamon and sugar

buffalo wings – despite the name this is actually chicken wings, marinated in a spicy sauce, and then either fried or grilled as a snack (photo right)

butter tart – a pioneer pastry tart with a butter, syrup and sugar filling. These small, individual tarts are considered to be one of the few genuinely Canadian recipes

Caesar – a drink made of vodka and clam juice served with celery and lime in a celery salt rimmed glass

cedar planked salmon – salmon that is grilled on a water soaked plank of cedar

clam/seafood chowder – hearty cream-based mussel/fish soup

Dungeness crab – large species of crab prized for its very sweet meat

hash browns – finely grated potatoes that are pan fried

Nanaimo bar – a rich dessert bar that originated in Nanaimo, BC

Pacific salmon – there are numerous different species such as Sockeye, Pink, Chum, Coho and Chinook – a popular dish in many restaurants

poutine – potato chips topped with curd cheese cubes and doused with gravy

Saskatoon berries – native to the Canadian prairies and British Columbia, they are similar to blueberries

scallops – shown in the left image

grilled in the Native American way – on planks of cedar – and dessert is ice cream with wild berries.

Your best bet for *breakfast* is in a coffee shop. Some of them are part of the hotel or are situated close to the motels. You can either enjoy a small continental breakfast or order a large American breakfast with eggs and fried potatoes, or pancakes which are usually served with maple syrup. Coffee is filled up free of charge, but often it is a watery brew. For *lunch*, roughly between noon and 2pm, the Canadians often eat smaller dishes, which are listed on a separate lunch menu, often a simple salad or soup and sandwich. In the rural regions, *dinner* is often served early between 5.30pm and 7pm, in the larger cities between 7pm and 10pm. In most restaurants you will need to wait to be shown you to your table. (A sign at the entrance will often tell you: 'Please wait to be seated'.)

After dinner the final amount of the bill may not be what you anticipated: the prices shown on the menu do not include the *tax*, which differs from province to province and it is only shown on the bill. The tip is also usually not included and if you are happy with the service then a 15–20 per cent tip is the norm.

There are also some local chains in addition to the global American *fast food chains*: *Earls* and the *Cactus Club are* popular restaurant chains in the greater Vancouver area that offer excellent dishes ranging from pasta to steaks and omelettes. *The Keg* chain is famous for good (but not exactly cheap) steaks. One of the branches of *Triple O White Spot* is a good choice if you long for a hamburger. They serve good quality food at reasonable prices and freshly bake their donuts and serve deliciously sweet milkshakes. Many Canadians pop into a *Tim Hortons* for a quick shot of sugar energy. The coffee and doughnut chain is more popular than Starbucks and serves good coffee and freshly baked doughnuts; they also offer affordable soups and sandwiches.

If there is a *national drink* in Canada, then it is beer – aromatic and very palatable, especially when compared to the rather watery American beer – which goes well with a hearty steak. Everywhere in the country you will find *Molson Canadian* or *Labatt's Blue,* while specialty beers such as *Kokanee* are served only in some regions. In recent years *micro breweries* have also become increasingly popular. In British Columbia you should try the beers by *Okanagan Spring* and *Granville Island Camp.* In Alberta, try beers by the *Wild*

Rose Brewing Company from Calgary. Many of the smaller places such as Canmore and Jasper have their own small breweries.

Wine is served in most restaurants; good wines from California or France are often listed. You should definitely try the local wines from the Okanagan Valley or the Niagara Peninsula. If you like it stronger, go for the excellent Canadian whiskey, which is either served on the rocks or – just like rum or gin – in mixed drinks. A specialty of the north is *Yukon Jack,* a devastatingly strong whiskey liqueur ideal for the long, cold winter nights.

In addition to the usual hotel bars there are also many rustic bars with a pool table and a long bar counter: often the best place to meet the locals. A West Canadian feature is the *cabaret*, not the usual kind of cabaret, instead the venue is a large bar and the performance is a country and western band.

Canadians love Tim Hortons' fast food

SHOPPING

Western Canada is not necessarily a well known shopping destination, but once you arrive you will be enticed by the wide selection of goods available. In the cities there is an excellent variety of shops, in the hinterland, however, your options decrease dramatically. A small grocery store that also sells shoes and chainsaws, or a gas station with a few shelves of items has to suffice in the small little towns. It is best to stock your camper with groceries and equipment before you go on a long trip. The further north you go the more expensive everything becomes.

CHEAP & TRENDY

Casual wear, sports shoes and sporting goods are much cheaper here than in Europe – even more so if the exchange rate is in your favour. The outlet shopping that is so popular in North America is still widely unknown in Western Canada, with the exception of a few malls in the region between Calgary and Edmonton.

The Canadian chain *Winners* has branches in many of the cities and specialises in discount sales of old stock, they have cheap jeans and children's clothing. Canadian sportswear brands such as *Lululemon Athletica* and *Roots Canada* are very popular with the fashion-conscious youth, but they are more expensive.

CULINARY

Regional products such as jam or wine from the Okanagan Valley, wild flower honey from the prairies or smoked salmon are popular souvenirs. There is also salmon served in unusual ways such as tinned smoked mousse or the delicious *Indian Candy*, salmon that has been candied and smoked. The most famous Canadian souvenir is maple syrup. The thickened sap from maple trees usually comes from the deciduous forests in the eastern regions and is an essential part of a hearty pancake breakfast in Canada.

MALLS & OLD TOWN DISTRICT

Shopping malls, departments stores and boutiques are everywhere in the major cities. Renovated old harbour waterfront districts are ideal for strolling and shopping such as Granville

Native American and Inuit carvings and sculptures are popular – and expensive – but there are other options too

Island in Vancouver or the old town district Victoria with restaurants, art galleries and cafés.

NATIVE AMERICAN ART

Native American and Inuit arts and crafts are popular but not cheap, the best option is to buy directly in the reservations, in reputable galleries or in the shops of the major museums. The west coast tribes, who were once famous for their totem poles, today carve smaller objects such as masks or bowls and also use the traditional stylised animal symbols that can be found in their art in silver jewellery and drawings. Native Americans in the northern regions traditionally make moccasins from moose leather, woven baskets decorated with porcupine quills as well as beaded leather jackets.

The Inuit of the Arctic are famous for their beautiful sculptures made from soapstone, whalebone and caribou antlers, which are sold in the galleries of the large cities (at prices from about C$300).

REGIONAL GIFTS

In the coastal villages of Vancouver Island and in Vancouver, you will find the beautiful, chunky Cowichan sweaters and all kinds of handicrafts items made of wood, clay and ceramic. Many artists, who usually exhibit their works in the galleries of Victoria, live mainly on the Gulf Islands off Vancouver Island. Ideal souvenirs from Alberta are cowboy items such as top quality Stetson hats, silver belt buckles and handmade boots. Many shops offer a good selection to choose from and you can even have a pair of boots custom-made. All over Alberta and British Columbia you will also find traditional checked lumberjack shirts that are good during the trip for protection against mosquito bites.

VANCOUVER

MAP INSIDE BACK COVER

There's no better start for a round trip through the West than Vancouver (144–145 C–D5) (𝄢 F14).

Vancouver is a young, vibrant city with a captivating charm and casual, European flair, a dynamic metropolis set against a dramatic backdrop of dark green mountains in the broad river delta of the Fraser River, with restored Victorian homes, spacious parks, beaches and plenty of unspoilt nature in the surrounding countryside.

With approximately 2.5 million inhabitants (the greater metropolitan area of the Fraser Delta), Vancouver is today the largest city in Western Canada. The city's more than 150 km/93 mi of port facilities makes it the most important economic and commercial centre on the

CITY WHERE TO START?

Start at the central square **Robson Square (U C–D4),** The Robson Street shopping district starts toward the west and further north is the old town around Water Street, Canada Place and the waterfront promenade Seawall at the Burrard Inlet. Within walking distance are Yaletown and the beaches in the West End close to Denman Street and Stanley Park. Parking garage in the Pacific Centre Mall at Robson/Granville Street. The next Skytrain Stations are Granville and City Centre.

Jewel of the Pacific: between the ocean and a breathtaking mountain backdrop lies the cultural metropolis of Western Canada

Pacific coast. Three renowned universities, numerous museums, theatres and galleries also make it the cultural hub of the region. In recent years so many films and TV shows have been shot in the city that it now has the nickname of 'Hollywood North'.

When Captain George Vancouver discovered the mouth of the Fraser River on the Pacific coast in 1792 – where he stayed only a short while and soon sailed on – there were only huge Douglas fir forests. Years later, in 1860, a small logging camp was established on the shores of Burrard Inlet. In 1886, when it became the terminal station of the transcontinental railway, Vancouver took off.

During the Olympic Winter Games in 2010 the city showcased what she had become: a liveable, natural metropolis, an oasis of fine urban culture in the midst of the wilderness of Western Canada. Set aside at least two days to explore Vancouver: one for an extended stroll through the city centre and one for a trip to the attractions in the city's outskirts.

Where is that smoke coming from? A steam clock tells the time in the historical Gastown quarter

SIGHTSEEING

A good initial overview of the city is to be had from the *The Lookout* tower on top of the *Harbour Centre* (U E3) (*e3*) on Hastings Street or – even better – a gondola ride on the aerial tramway system up *Grouse Mountain* with spectacular views of the city. Back on the ground, explore the city on foot or by rental bicycle. *Vancouver Trolleys (daily 9–6pm | fare C$47)* offers two guided bus tours along fixed routes that cover all city attractions. Hop on and off as you wish as you can catch a bus every 20 minutes.

BILL REID GALLERY (U D3) (*d3*)

Not especially big but very interesting: works of the famous Native American artist, who died in 1998. *Daily 10am–5pm, winter closed Mon/Tue | admission C$11 | 639 Hornby St.*

CANADA PLACE ★ (U E3) (*e3*)

During the Expo 86 the pier, with its snow-white tent design by architect Ed Zeidler, was the Canada Pavilion. It's perfect for a stroll, to watch cruise ships coming and going and to enjoy the view over the fjord from the top of the pier *(Cordova St./Howe St.)*. The grassed flat roofed building next door, constructed in 2010 with sustainable technologies, demonstrates Vancouver's aim to be Canada's 'greenest' city: It's the gigantic hall of the International Media Centre for the Olympic Games, which today is the *Vancouver Convention Centre.* The *Olympic Torch* on its west side reminds of the winter games.

CAPILANO SALMON HATCHERY ● (144 C5) (*F14*)

Here you can view the life cycle of salmon through underwater gallery windows and information panels. From mid August, the adult salmon return. *Daily in summer 8am–8pm | admission free | North Vancouver | Capilano Rd.*

CAPILANO SUSPENSION BRIDGE (144 C5) (*F14*)

A swaying, almost 140 m/459 ft long suspension bridge spans the 70 m/229.7 ft deep canyon. There is also a totem pole park, a nature trail in the treetops and a spectacular cliff walk high above the gorge. However, this tourist attraction draws crowds of visitors. *Daily in summer 8.30am–8pm, otherwise 9am–5pm | admission C$43 | North Vancouver | Capilano Rd.*

CHINATOWN (U F4) *(𝄐 f4)*

Around Pender and Main Street is the busy and somewhat grubby old Chinatown of Vancouver, which again has become trendy in recent years with hot spots and clubs. Worth seeing is the *Dr. Sun Yat-Sen Classical Chinese Garden* on Carr Street. On Friday to Sunday evenings there is the *Night Market* around Main/Keefer Street with many stalls. Also well worth a visit is the modern INSIDERTIP *T & T Supermarket (Keefer St./Abbott St.)* which offers every imaginable Asian product. The area of Hastings Street nearby has lots of vagrants – it is not dangerous, but also not very nice.

GASTOWN (U E4) *(𝄐 e4)*

This district is the restored old town of Vancouver, its boundary runs along Water Street. Today, the old brick buildings house shops, restaurants and art galleries. A fun attraction is the *Steam Clock* on the corner of Cambie Street, which is powered by steam from the municipal heating network. A statue of city founder John 'Gassy Jack' Deighton is just east at the Water/Carr Street intersection. It is assumed that he was the one who built the first house in Vancouver in 1867 – a saloon. This established a tradition and today there are still numerous pubs around the square.

GRANVILLE ISLAND
(U B–C6) *(𝄐 b–c6)*

The restored waterfront harbour area under the Granville Bridge is another attractive area in Vancouver: do some shopping at the famous ● *Public Market*, browse colourful art shops like the *Gallery of BC Ceramics (1359 Cartwright St.)* or eat ice cream with a view of houseboats and city skyline. Not to be missed: INSIDERTIP Railspur Alley with artist studios, innovative galleries and a small café.

MARITIME MUSEUM (U A5) *(𝄐 a5)*

The jewel in the museum's crown is the 'St Roch', an Arctic patrol ship. The wooden schooner traversed the Northwest Passage several times. *June–Sept daily 10am–5pm, Thu till 8pm, otherwise Tue–Sat, Sun only from noon | admission C$12.50 | 1100 Chestnut St.*

STANLEY PARK ★ (U A–D1) *(𝄐 a–d1)*

A beautiful urban park with hiking trails and picnic areas where there are some original totem poles surrounded by a dense forest of ancient Douglas

---

MARCO POLO HIGHLIGHTS

★ **Canada Place**
Built for Expo 86 and now a hub of activity with harbour promenade, cafés and great views → p. 34

★ **Stanley Park**
The most beautiful urban park in Canada – ideal for a bike ride → p. 35

★ **UBC Museum of Anthropology**
Original totem poles and masks of the Northwest Coast Native Americans → p. 36

★ **Bridges**
Popular meeting place in the late afternoon – views over the water and chic clientele → p. 37

firs. Built in 1938 the *Lions Gate Bridge,* at the northern tip of the park, connects the city to North Vancouver. The 1000 acre park also incorporates the ● *Vancouver Aquarium* with dolphins, fur seals, sea otters, and an exhibition on the migration of salmon *(daily in summer 9.30am–6pm, otherwise 10am–5pm | admission C$39).* You can

10am–9pm, Oct–mid May closed Mon | admission C$18 | 6393 NW Marine Dr.

VANCOUVER MUSEUM (U A5) *(ᗰ a5)*

The large Rotunda on the shore of English Bay exhibits the history of the city of Vancouver, the natural history of the area as well as Native American craftwork. Adjacent is the *MacMillan Space*

Bill Reid allowed himself to become inspired by the legends of his ancestors: Museum of Anthropology

cycle around the peninsula, on which the park is situated, on the 10 km/ 6.2 mi long ☃ ● *Stanley Park Drive (bicycle rental near the Denman St. entrance | C$23–49 for half a day).*

UBC MUSEUM OF ANTHROPOLOGY ★
(144 C5) *(ᗰ F14)*

The unconventional museum building by Arthur Erickson, in the grounds of the University of British Columbia, houses an important collection of totem poles and masks of the Northwest Coast Native Americans. Beautiful historic carvings from Argyllit as well as modern works by Bill Reid. *Daily in summer 10am–5pm, Thu*

Centre & Planetarium, with evening laser shows. *Daily 10am–5pm, Thu 10am–8pm, Fri/Sat until 9pm | admission C$19 | 1100 Chestnut St.*

VAN DUSEN BOTANICAL GARDEN
(144 C5) *(ᗰ F14)*

Covers 55 acres and is full of plants, flowers, groves, idyllic paths and small lakes. The garden is particularly colourful from May to July. *Daily 9am–sunset, in winter from 10am | admission C$11| 5251 Oak St.*

INSIDER TIP ▶ YALETOWN (U D5) *(ᗰ d5)*

The city's trendy district: during the day the quirky boutiques along Hamilton and

Mainland Street attract visitors, and then at night it is the chic restaurants, brew pubs and bars.

FOOD & DRINK

BRIDGES ⭐ �► (U B6) (𝛺 b6)
Lovely bistro with a large terrace on the water and wonderful views of the city. *1696 Duranleau St. | Granville Island | tel. 604 6 87 44 00 | www.bridgesres taurant.com | Budget–Expensive*

INSIDER TIP CACAO (U A6) (𝛺 a6)
South America meets Canada: the Venezuelan Jefferson Alvarez sends out food worthy of stars from the kitchen: octopus with pineapple salsa and delicious yucca chips! Reservation necessary! *1898 W 1st Ave. | tel. 604 7 31 53 70 | www.cacaovancouver.com | Moderate–Expensive*

CAFFE ARTIGIANO
(U D3) (𝛺 d3)
Popular café chain with excellent cappuccino, breakfast and snacks; there are branches at *1101 W Pender St.* and *740 W Hastings St. | Budget*

EDIBLE CANADA 🌐
(U B65) (𝛺 b5)
Trendy organic bistro with terrace and shop. Delicious fish tacos from their street stall, and if you arrive in an electric car, there is a charging station right outside the door. *1596 Johnston St. | Granville Island | tel. 604 6 82 66 81 | www.ediblecanada.com | Moderate*

DINESTY (U B2) (𝛺 b2)
Modern Chinese restaurant in the young West end of the inner city; excellent Shanghai dumplings. *1719 Robson St. | tel. 604 6 69 77 69 | Moderate*

INSIDER TIP KINGYO (U B2) (𝛺 b2)
Japanese restaurant popular with the young Asian set, serving amazing creations. *871 Denman St. | tel. 604 6 08 16 77 | www.kingyo-izakaya.ca | Moderate*

THE SANDBAR (U C6) (𝛺 c6)
Excellent fish served in all variations, large bar and INSIDER TIP heated rooftop terrace with fireplace, above False Creek. *1535 Johnston St. | Granville Island | tel. 604 6 69 90 30 | Moderate*

TAPSHACK �► (U C2) (𝛺 c2)
Ideal for a break on the promenade Coal Harbour. *1199 W Cordova St. | tel. 604 6 87 64 55 | Budget–Moderate*

SHOPPING

The main shopping street is the lively *Robson Street*. The Bay is north of the Robson Square. *Granville Island* and the *Lonsdale Quay Market* are also popular for their stalls, cafés, and quirky shops.

FINEST AT SEA SEAFOOD BOUTIQUE
(U B6) (𝛺 b6)
Excellent wild salmon: smoked, frozen, canned and of course the unique *Salmon Candy. 1805 Mast Tower Rd. | Granville Island | www.finestatsea.com*

ENTERTAINMENT

Listing for current concerts and clubs are in the weekly publication 'Georgia Straight', the monthly magazine 'Where Vancouver', as well as in the weekend edition of the 'Vancouver Sun'. Tickets for concerts, theatre shows and sporting events are available at *Tickets Tonight* in the *Vancouver Tourist Info Centre (Waterfront Centre | 200 Burrard St. | www.ticketstonight.ca)*. (U D4) (𝛺 d4) The downtown nightlife focuses on Gastown with good pubs such as the *Portside Pub (7 Alexander St.)* or the *Charles Bar (136 Cordova St.),* in West End around *Davie* and *Denman St.* as well as in the historic old warehouses of vibrant and trendy *Yaletown* (U D5) (*泣 d5*). There is also the popular brew pub *Yaletown Brewing Co. (1111 Mainland St., with restaurant)*. On weekends the youth queue up in front of the many clubs on *Granville Street* (U D4) (*泣 d4*), and meet in the *Commodore Ballroom* to enjoy reggae, deep house, funk *(868 Granville St.)*.

CENTURY PLAZA (U C4) (*泣 c4*)
A comfortable mid range hotel within walking distance of Robson Street. The spa is also open to non-guests. *236 rooms | 1015 Burrard St. | tel. 604 6 87 05 75 | www.centuryplaza.com | Moderate*

FAIRMONT WATERFRONT 〰 (U D3) (*泣 d3*)
Luxury hotel in a prime location between the harbour and Gastown, with beautiful views over the Burrard Inlet. *489 rooms | 900 Canada Place Way | tel. 604 6 91 19 91 | www.fairmont.com | Expensive*

LISTEL VANCOUVER (U C3) (*泣 c3*)
Art-style hotel in the heart of the city with a restaurant offering excellent west coast cuisine. *129 rooms | 1300 Robson St. | tel. 604 6 84 84 61 | www.thelistelhotel.com | Moderate–Expensive*

INSIDER TIP ▶ SYLVIA (U A3) (*泣 a3*)
Older, charming mid range hotel in West End, right on English Bay beach. *119 rooms | 1154 Gilford St. | tel. 604 6 81 93 21 | www.sylviahotel.com | Budget–Moderate*

ECOMARINE PADDLING CENTRE (U B5) (*泣 b5*)
Centre for the rental of kayaks and SUP (stand up paddle) boards for customised tours on False Creek. Courses and guided tours. Rental: C$19–39 for 2 hours. *1668 Duranleau St. | Granville Island | tel. 604 6 89 75 75 | www.ecomarine.com*

BEACHES
Though the waters of the Pacific Ocean are relatively chilly even in summer, the

English Bay Beach: Vancouver's most popular beach close to the city's centre

beaches of *English Bay* are nice for a quick dip and some sunbathing. The beaches *Kitsilano* (beach volleyball) and *Jericho* located west of the city centre are best.

INFORMATION

VANCOUVER TOURIST CENTRE
(U D3) (*₪ d3*)
Multilingual staff. Accommodation service, tickets, sightseeing tours. *Waterfront Centre | 200 Burrard St. | tel. 604 6 83 22 22 | www.tourismvancouver.com*

WHERE TO GO

LANGLEY (145 D5) (*₪ F14*)
INSIDERTIP *Fort Langley National Historic Site* (*daily in July and Aug 9am–5pm, otherwise 10am–5pm | admission C$7.80*), the old fur trading fort on the Fraser River, is located approximately 50 km/31.1 mi east of Hwy. 1, and is today a museum village. The 'inhabitants' of the old trading post guide you through the harsh lifestyle of the trappers in the 19th century.

Fort Langley town itself also deserves a stroll. The picturesque main street, Glover Road, is lined with shady trees, numerous antique shops, boutiques and pleasant restaurants such as the *Lamplighter Café. 9213 Glover Rd | tel. 604 8 88 64 64 | Moderate*

RICHMOND (144–145 C–D5) (*₪ F14*)
About half an hour south of the city centre (you can also take the *Canada Line* metro rail) is Vancouver's Chinese neighbourhood. Innumerable Asian restaurants line No. 3 Road, and near by, on the banks of the Fraser River, is the distinctive *Richmond Oval*, venue of the Olympic speed skating events.

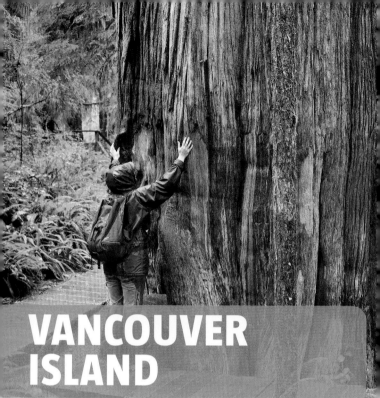

VANCOUVER ISLAND

Vancouver Island is the largest (450 km/280 mi) island on the west coast of North America and it is a world in its own. A fascinating primeval landscape of deep fjords and high mountains, laced with peaceful bays and spectacular beaches waits to be explored by its visitors.

The island's rewards are in its contrasts: sleepy fishing villages, Native American reserves and lumberjack camps in the isolated north, bustling holiday villages and the elegant capital Victoria in the south. But above all, the island is an ideal destination for those who like to have a holiday in and with nature.

To date only one road leads along the whole island, Highway 19, the north-south thoroughfare. For the majority of the distance it runs along on the eastern coast, protected by a long stretch of mountain massif. The wild, rainy western coast – which is home to the Pacific Rim National Park with its unique rain forests and rugged rocks – is still almost inaccessible and thus an ideal destination for wilderness hikers and kayakers.

The mild eastern coast, however, is very accessible and is known for its bathing beaches – the shallow waters of the Strait of Georgia, which separates the island from the Mainland, are pleasantly warm in the summer.

Island information: *Tourism Vancouver Island | Information Centre on Hwy. 4 at Tofino | tel. 250 7 54 35 00 | www.vancouverisland.travel*

Whales and rain forests, unspoilt beaches and verdant fjords – these are the many and varied charms of the west coast

CAMPBELL RIVER

(144 B4) (*E13*) **It's an anglers' paradise. This port city (pop. 35,000) is among the largest cities on Vancouver Island.**

The largest salmon in Canada are caught in the central part of the island. King Salmon weighing 30 kg/66.1 lbs. are not uncommon. During high season, the sound is full of boats. *Quadra Island,* a barrier island that can be reached by ferry, is a Kwakiutl Native American reserve. Here you find the INSIDER TIP *Nuyumbalees Cultural Centre (daily in summer 10am–4pm | admission C$10 | Cape Mudge),* a true treasure trove of Native American masks of the Kwakiutl. If you want to stay overnight then try the *Tsa-Kwa-Lu-ten Lodge (35 rooms | Quadra Island | tel. 250 2 85 20 42 | www.capemudgeresort. bc.ca | Moderate–Expensive),* a lodge (with campsite) run by Native Americans and decorated with carvings. Another

in the park up into the alpine regions. *Golden Hinde* is the highest mountain at 2500 m/8202 ft. Especially beautiful is the hike to *Flower Ridge* at the southern end of the *Buttle Lake.* On the banks of the Upper Campbell Lake is the cosy *Strathcona Park Lodge (46 rooms, holiday homes and chalets | tel. 250 2 86 31 22 | www.strathconaparklodge. com | Moderate)* which offers hiking, mountaineering and canoeing.

DUNCAN

(144 C5) (⌘ E14) The town (pop. 5000) in the fertile Cowichan Valley was not particularly special until the Cowichan Native Americans on the adjacent reserve founded a cultural centre to honour their traditions and began to carve totem poles.

The village is dotted with brightly painted poles – widely appreciated by the locals in town as they attract tourists and bring in the money.

Cowichan totem poles in Duncan

option is a modern, small hotel with sea views and good location close to the harbour 🌿 *Heron's Landing (3 rooms | 492 South Island Hwy. | tel. 250 9 23 28 48 | www.heronslandinghotel.com | Budget– Moderate).*

WHERE TO GO

STRATHCONA PROV. PARK
(144 B4–5) (⌘ D–E 13–14)
The oldest provincial park in British Columbia, 50 km/31.1 mi west of Campbell River, is especially interesting for hikers. It has a well developed network of paths leading from the two roads

SIGHTSEEING

B. C. FOREST DISCOVERY CENTER
This where everything has to do with logging and lumberjacks – from old chain saws to a sawmill to a real lumberjack camp – you can explore everything in this open-air museum. *Daily in summer 10am–4.30pm | admission C$16 and includes a ride on an old steam train | 2892 Drinkwater Rd. | www.bcforestdiscovery centre.com*

COWICHAN BAY MARITIME CENTRE
Boat museum spread among several small houses at the harbour. Also a good place to visit with children. *Open in summer 8.30am-4.30pm | admission free | 1761 Cowichan Bay Rd.*

FOOD & DRINK

INSIDER TIP GENOA BAY CAFE

It is somewhat located somewhere out of the way on a secluded and idyllic bay, but the trip is well worth the extra time to get there. *5000 Genoa Bay Rd. | tel. 250 7 46 76 21 | Moderate*

WHERE TO GO

PORT RENFREW (144 C5) (*E14*)

From Duncan, take the recently opened and paved Hwy. 18 that leads 150 km/93 mi via Lake Cowichan and the densely forested mountains to Port Renfrew on the west coast. The small, secluded village sits on the southern edge of the *Pacific Rim National Park* (the starting point for the West Coast Trail) and offers a long beach and camping in the adjacent Native American reserve. Don't miss the **INSIDER TIP** *Botanical Beach* with its bizarre rock formations and diverse marine flora found in large pools formed by the tides (make sure you know ahead of time when the tide is low). Continue on Hwy. 14 from Port Renfrew to Victoria and you will have completed a round trip of the southern part of Vancouver Island.

NANAIMO

(144 C5) (*E14*) **Nanaimo is the northern ferry port for the ships to the mainland and a good starting point for tours to the central part of the island.**

Well-kept parks with amazing yacht harbours and an attractive harbour promenade: the second-largest town (pop. 90,000) on Vancouver Island is very beautiful. Nanaimo has gained a reputation over the last few years as a diving location. The extremely clear water gives you a great chance of discovering wrecks and a diverse underwater flora.

SPORTS & ACTIVITIES

WILDPLAY NANAIMO

Adventure park for both adults and children: bungee jumps, zip lining, rope climbing section – all with plenty of adrenaline. *Prices from C$30 | 35 Nanaimo River Rd. | tel. 855 5 95 22 51 | www.wildplay.com*

WHERE TO STAY

BUCCANEER INN 🌊

Comfortable and eco-conscious motel near the ferry port. Good base for divers. *14 rooms | 1577 Stewart Ave. | tel. 250 7 53 12 46 | www.buccaneerinn.com | Moderate*

★ **Pacific Rim National Park**
Ancient trees, rain forests and wild, pristine beaches along the west coast → p. 44

★ **Inside Passage**
Silent fjords, deep blue water: the most beautiful coast in all of Canada → p. 46

★ **Stubbs Island Whale Watching**
See the pods of magnificent killer whales → p. 47

★ **Inner Harbour**
Hustle and bustle, yachts and large flower pots hanging from the street lamps → p. 48

MARCO POLO HIGHLIGHTS

WHERE TO GO

GULF ISLANDS
(144–145 C–D 5–6) *(ⅢⅢ E–F 14)*

A whole archipelago of small islands lies between Vancouver Island and the mainland. *Saltspring*, *Galiano* and *Gabriola* are the most important among them – they are accessible by ferry from Swartz Bay, Crofton or Nanaimo. The grand nature and its mild and sunny climate – you can even find palm trees! – attracted artists, writers and artisans. The best way to explore the islands is by bicycle: you can travel quickly from island to island by ferry and on some of the islets – where certain parts are car-free – a bicycle is the best means of transport.

PARKSVILLE (144 C5) *(ⅢⅢ E14)*

The charm of Nanaimo lies in the surrounding area: around 25 km/15.5 mi to the north, around Parksville and *Qualicum Beach* there are some very attractive beaches with warm waters. A 20 minute drive inland on Hwy. 4 leads to the *MacMillan Provincial Park* where you can marvel at the 800 year old Douglas firs and cedar trees, or the cascades of *Little Qualicum Falls* (hiking trails). You can then stay the night at *Tigh-Na-Mara Resort (192 rooms | 1155 Resort Dr. | tel. 250 2 48 20 72 | www.tigh-na-mara.com | Moderate–Expensive)* with log cabins and apartments right on the beach and a large spa with mineral pool and ⊙seaweed, clay and sea salt organic wraps.

PACIFIC RIM NAT. PARK

(144 B–C 5–6) (ⅢⅢ D–E14) ★ ● **The wildest and most beautiful sections of the coast form part of this 150 mi²**

nature reserve. The park protects an ancient rain forest, rugged cliffs and driftwood-strewn beaches, such as the 11 km/6.8 mi aptly named Long Beach. The *Kwisitis Centre* on ⊱ *Wickaninnish Beach* provides very detailed and competent information on the natural history of the region. The friendly and helpful rangers will give you valuable tips for hikes. The nature trails are particularly impressive, such as the *Rainforest Trail*, and given the weather conditions in the area it is a good idea to equip yourself with a waterproof cape.

The small archipelago of the *Broken Group Islands* is a great destination for wilderness kayakers, and if the weather conditions are good then hikers should book the week-long *West Coast Trail* (75 km/46.6 mi long and reservation required, *tel. 519 8 26 53 91*) from Port Renfrew to Bamfield. Highly recommended is also the ● *Wild Pacific Trail* in the southern town of *Ucluelet*, which stretches across three sub-sections of the rugged coast. From *Tofino*, the small port city on the northern edge of the park, you can take boat trips to secluded coves and go whale watching in the *Clayoquot Sound*. It is also very popular to go INSIDERTIP► bear watching from a boat. This is a safe way to observe the predators.

SPORTS & ACTIVITIES

ATLEO RIVER AIR SERVICE

This are organised tours by seaplane across glaciers, fjords and waterfalls. *50 Wingen Lane | tel. 866 6 62 85 36 | www. atleoair.com*

BARKLEY SOUND SERVICE

A former Norwegian freight ferry offers cruises in the Barkley Sound. Full day trips from Port Alberni to Ucluelet and

Bamfield. They also transport hikers to the *West Coast Trail* and kayakers to the *Broken Group Islands* (book in advance). *Port Alberni | tel. 250 7 23 83 13 | www. ladyrosemarine.com*

REMOTE PASSAGES
Motorboat and rubber dingy trips to observe grey whales, orca and bears and to the hot springs on a secluded island. *51 Wharf St. | tel. 250 7 25 33 30 | www. remotepassages.com*

SURF SISTER
Ride a wave for an exciting adrenaline rush: in spite of the name they offer both women-only and mixed courses. A trial course, including board and wetsuit, costs about C$85. *625 Campbell St. | tel. 250 7 25 44 56 | www.surfsister.com*

FOOD & DRINK

NORWOODS
Creative west coast cuisine in a cosy restaurant decorated with lots of wood. The ingredients, such as mussels or Dungeness crab, are supplied by local fishermen, who rely on sustainable catch. *1714 Peninsula Rd. | Ucluelet | tel. 250 7 26 70 01 | Moderate–Expensive*

SHELTER
Try the salmon and halibut in a Macadamia crust, or the pork chops in apple sauce. Very good: Dungeness crab, fresh from the west coast. *601 Campbell St. | tel. 250 7 25 33 53 | Moderate*

SOBO
Delicious, very healthy west coast cuisine. The lunchtime menu is very reasonably priced. *311 Neill St. | tel. 250 7 25 23 41 | Expensive*

WHERE TO STAY

HETINKIS LODGE
Three luxurious apartments in a wonderful location on a rock fringed bay. *Ucluelet | tel. 250 7 26 29 28 | www.hetinkis lodge. com | Moderate–Expensive*

INSIDER TIP LONG BEACH LODGE
This could be your own chic lodge right on the beach, including surf school and

Encounter at Clayoquot Sound: black bears in the Pacific Rim National Park

a good restaurant. Many of the rooms overlook the sea. Ideal for families. *41 rooms, 20 cottages | 1441 Pacific Rim Hwy. | tel. 250 7 25 24 42 | www.long beachlodgeresort.com | Expensive*

WHALERS ON THE POINT GUESTHOUSE ☆

Cosy hostel in the centre of the village, the ideal base for surfers, backpackers and active vacationers. *4–6 bed dorm rooms and 4 double rooms | 81 West St. Tofino | tel. 250 7 25 34 43 | www.tofino hostel.com | Budget*

PORT HARDY

(144 A3–4) (*ψ D12–13*) The busy port is evidence that the town (pop. 4000), in the wild north of Vancouver Island, is an important fishing base.

Port Hardy is liked by visitors as it is a good starting point for the *Inside Passage* and other rewarding trips: you can see whales, bears and eagles on kayak, take hikes to Cape Scott, flights and boat trips.

WHERE TO STAY

GLEN LYON INN ☆

Comfortable hotel with beautiful harbour views and, if you are lucky, you may spot a bald eagle from your window. Good in-house pub/restaurant. *44 rooms | 6435 Hardy Bay Rd. | tel. 250 9 49 71 15 | www. glenlyoninn.com | Budget–Moderate*

INSIDER TIP GREAT BEAR LODGE ◉

A floating eco lodge that is the base for grizzly bear and nature observation tours. Great location on a fjord on the mainland coast. Access is by seaplane from Port Hardy. *tel. 250 9 49 94 96 | www.great beartours.com | Moderate–Expensive*

WHERE TO GO

ALERT BAY (144 B4) (*ψ D13*)

The village (pop. 600) on a small off-shore island around 40 km/24.9 mi south on Hwy. 19 (ferry from Port Mc-Neill) is home to the Kwakwaka'wakw Native Americans *(Kwakiutl)*, famous for their particularly expressive carving. The most beautiful heirlooms of the tribe – old masks, decorated chests and totem poles – are exhibited in the INSIDER TIP *U' Mista Cultural Centre (daily in summer 9am–5pm, otherwise only Tue–Sat | admission C$12 | www.umista.ca | guided tours organised by the Culture Shock Gallery on the ferry port | tel. 250 9 74 24 84 | www. cultureshockgallery.ca)*. For a night right on the river, try the *Seine Boat Inn (10 rooms | tel. 877 334 94 65 | www. seineboatinn.com | Budget–Moderate)*.

INSIDE PASSAGE ★ ● ☆
(144 A–C 3–4) (*ψ D–E 12–14*)

The 500 km/311 mi long coastal shipping route runs along the west coast, and was once the route followed by of thousands of adventurers on their way to the gold fields of Klondike and to Alaska. There are still no roads along the coast, which is lined by numerous fjords. The only way

Inside Passage: legendary waterway along the many islands of the west coast of British Columbia

to experience the legendary route is by cruise ship (from Vancouver) or on one of the *BC Ferries* on a 15 hour trip between *Port Hardy* and *Prince Rupert* (you will need to book several months in advance, information on site at *tel. 888 2 23 37 79, www.bcferries.com).*

TELEGRAPH COVE (144 B4) (⟋ D13)

The former fishing hamlet (pop. 20), less than an hour's drive south of Port Hardy, is now a Mecca for whale watchers and researchers. Several groups of orca live here in the salmon-rich waters of a marine reserve (between the mainland and Vancouver Island) and they can be seen here throughout the summer. Half-day boat tours are on offer between May to October by ★ ⋆ *Stubbs Island Whale Watching (Telegraph Cove | price C$133 | tel. 800 6 65 30 66 | www.stubbs-island.com)* to Johnstone Strait, an Orca reservation.

Also full-day boat trips are offered from Telegraph Cove to the grizzlies in *Knight Inlet*. The bears can often be seen up close from a boat in the secluded fjord near the mainland. Tours are organised by *Tide Rip Tours (daily tour C$320–360 | tel. 250 3 39 53 20 | www.grizzlycanada.com)* from June to September.

VICTORIA

(144 C6) (⟋ E15) **Victoria (pop. 370,000), since 1871 capital of British Columbia, basks in the colonial legacy of the British Empire – with landscaped public parks, Victorian architecture, doubledecker buses and horse-drawn carriages for sightseeing.**

A stylish English tea in the ivy-covered Fairmont Empress Hotel (a landmark dating from 1906) is a tradition in the city. The mild climate (ideal for golf enthusiasts) and its location on the waters of the Juan de Fuca Strait make Victoria one of the most popular resorts in the west. It is now popular with

WHERE TO START?
Inner Harbour is the heart of the city; from here it is only a short walk to the Royal British Columbia Museum and to Parliament in the south and – in the north – to the old town on Government Street and Chinatown on Fisgard Street. Public parking is just north of Inner Harbour along Wharf Street.

Parliament Building is the seat of legislative authority

major attractions. On the eastern side is the famed *Fairmont Empress Hotel,* on the northern side is the *old town* with its shopping streets and small alleys, while to the south, in a commanding position, are the magnificent *Parliament Buildings* dating from 1898, with a statue of Queen Victoria. The best way to explore the harbour is to take a trip on one of the small *Harbour Ferry Company boats* *(round trip C$26 | departure from Empress Hotel | victoriaharbourferry.com).*

ROYAL BRITISH COLUMBIA MUSEUM

The largest museum in the province; the natural history section includes a micro rain forest and a tidal pool, the cultural section has magnificent totem poles and exhibitions about pioneer history. With IMAX cinema and shop. *Daily 10am–5pm | admission C$22, with IMAX C$32 | 675 Belleville St.*

well-heeled seniors who want to spend their retirement playing golf or a enjoying the extensive *Butchard Gardens* at the northern end of the city. It is also popular with students and young people who enjoy sailing and who appreciate the leisure activities of the city.

SIGHTSEEING

BEACON HILL PARK

The urban park is the site of the 'Mile 0' plaque (intersection of Douglas and Dallas Rd) that marks the start of the *Trans-Canada Highway* which runs 7821 km/4860 mi east in Newfoundland. From here you can take the ⚡ *Scenic Marine Drive* that follows the coast through suburbs such as Oak Bay.

INNER HARBOUR ★

No visit to Victoria is complete without a walk along the harbour basin, filled with sailboats and yachts, to some of the city's

TOURS

EAGLE WING TOURS ●

Whale watching with catamarans to the islands off the coast where several pods of orca live in summer. *3–4 hour tour C$135 | including pick-up at the hotel | departure from Fisherman's Wharf | 12 Erie St. | tel. 250 3 84 80 08 | www.eaglewingtours.com*

FOOD & DRINK

FLYING OTTER GRILL ⚡

Popular pub with a terrace on the harbour, surrounded by yachts and seaplanes; good for breakfast, lunch and dinner. *950 Wharf St. | tel. 250 4 14 42 20 | Moderate*

INSIDER TIP▸ MO:LÉ 🌐

A cosy coffee shop offering tasty multicultural cuisine, organic ingredients are used extensively. Only open for breakfast and lunch. *554 Pandora Ave. | tel. 250 3 85 66 53 | Budget–Moderate*

SWAN'S PUB AND CAFE
A popular pub in the city, serving salads and fresh fish, that is also a good option for an evening out. *506 Pandora St. | tel. 250 3 61 33 10 | Budget*

SHOPPING

MARKET SQUARE
The brick buildings of the beautifully renovated warehouses at the harbour are full of shops, art galleries and restaurants. *560 Johnson St.*

WHERE TO STAY

FAIRMONT EMPRESS
Steeped in traditional, but recently renovated. *464 rooms | 721 Government St. | tel. 250 3 84 81 11 | www.fairmont.com | Expensive*

HOTEL ZED
Modest but quirky design motel on the northern outskirts of the centre. Free rented bicycles. *62 rooms | 3110 Douglas St. | tel. 250 3 88 43 45 | www.hotelzed. com | Budget–Moderate*

INFORMATION

TOURISM VICTORIA
Information Office at Inner Harbour, they also help with accommodation. *812 Wharf St. | tel. 250 9 53 20 33 | www. tourismvictoria.com*

WHERE TO GO

FISGARD LIGHTHOUSE (144 C6) (*M E15*)
Ever since 1860, the picturesque lighthouse – the oldest on the Canadian West coast – has been guiding vessels into the harbour. It lies 15 km/9.3 mi further west of Victoria on Hwy. 1. From there, the highway continues westward to a real gourmet treat: ✂ *Sooke Harbour House (1528 Whiffen Spit Rd. | Sooke | tel. 250 6 42 34 21 | www.sookeharbour house.com | Moderate–Expensive, including 28 rooms | Expensive)*. It is perfectly located at a high spot above a small bay, provides great views and serves delicious regional cuisine.

INSIDER TIP ▶ SHAW CENTRE FOR THE SALISH SEA (144 C5) (*M E14*)
The underwater ecosystem of Canada's west coast of is the subject of this excellent, non-profit aquarium, half an hour's drive north of Victoria. *Daily 10am–4pm | admission C$17 | 9811 Seaport Place | Sidney*

LOW BUDGET

Ideal base for low budget tours to Vancouver Island is the Painted Turtle Guest House *(20 rooms | 121 Bastion St. | Nanaimo | tel. 866 3 09 44 32 | www.paintedturtle.ca)* in Nanaimo. The pleasantly restored building in the old town is an informal forum of information about lifts and tours. A bed in one of the dorms costs C$33; single rooms start at C$79.

A wilderness lodge on a secluded fjord need not be extremely expensive. On Quadra Island the ecologically run ✪ *Discovery Islands Lodge (8 beds | Surge narrows | tel. 250 2 85 28 23 | www.discovery-islands-lodge.com)* offers a double room incl. breakfast for C$110. Bring your own sleeping bag. Full day kayak tours cost C$110.

BRITISH COLUMBIA

British Columbia (generally abbreviated as BC) boastfully calls itself the most scenic province in Canada. And not without cause: the westernmost region of the country. Offers the largest variety of landscapes and therewith the best opportunities for an adventurous holiday.

Whether canoeing, hiking, heli-skiing, fishing, biking or white water rafting: BC has thrills and adventure to suit every taste. It even has sunny beaches and waters warm enough for swimming – such as the popular lakes in the Okanagan Valley.

The mainland of this large and fascinating province covers approximately 365,000 mi². The offshore island of Vancouver Island (→ p. 40) as well as the city of Vancouver (→ p. 32) both deserve their own chapter.

The entire region is characterised by large mountain ranges – not only by the Rockies that only start at the extreme eastern edge of the province – but by numerous other large mountain ranges that all form part of the North American Cordillera. Verdant mountains alternate with high plateaus into which rivers – such as the Fraser River – have cut broad valleys. Only the extreme northeast, the region around Dawson Creek, is flat. There, the province extends to the foothills of the prairie. And on the border with the United States at Osoyoos, you will find Canada's only desert – one that even includes cacti and rattlesnakes.

Between the Rockies and the Pacific: towering mountains, jewel-like lakes, fascinating pioneer towns – British Columbia has it all

CARIBOO REGION

(145 D–E 1–4) (*ﾉ F–G 11–13*) **The steppe-like plateau on the upper reaches of the Fraser River is Canada's own Wild West: hilly ranch country with large herds of cattle and gold rush towns.**

To supply miners during the great gold rush of 1860, the *Cariboo Wagon Road* was built. Hwy. 97 follows this old route.

Many of the small ranch villages were named after the distances from the original start of the road in *Lillooet* (145 D4) (*ﾉ E13*): *70 Mile House*, *100 Mile House* etc. The starting point for tours around *Barkerville*, *Likely* or *Horsefly* is *Williams Lake* (145 D2) (*ﾉ F12*).

SIGHTSEEING

BARKERVILLE (145 D1) (*ﾉ H11*)

During the 1870s, Barkerville was the largest city north of San Francisco. Today it's a INSIDER TIP wonderfully nostalgic museum village with wooden facades and sidewalks and actors enacting the pioneer lifestyle. Attractive restaurants: the historic *Wake-up Jake Café (tel. 250 9 94 32 59 | Moderate)* serves hearty gold digger food and the *Lung Duck Tong Restaurant (tel. 250 9 94 34 58 | Moderate)* serves delicious Chinese food. *Visitor centre with museum daily 8.30am–7pm | entry in summer C$20 | at the edge of the city on Hwy. 26 | www.barkerville.ca*

at festivals and you can make acquaintance with numerous talented actors within the creative scene, for example at *Island Mountain Arts (www.support-imarts.com)*.

WHERE TO STAY

BECKER'S LODGE (145 D1) (*⑳ G11*)
Lodge right on the lake, also chalets and camping. Equipment and rental for the week long canoe trips on the

Where many holiday dreams become reality: Clearwater Lake Lodge

COTTONWOOD HOUSE (145 D1) (*⑳ G11*)
A historic site in Cottonwood, a faithfully restored coach inn dating back to 1864, also horse-drawn carriage rides. *Daily in summer 10am–5pm | admission C$5 | on Hwy. 26*

WELLS (145 D1) (*⑳ G11*)
The old mining town on the western edge of the Cariboo Mountains has evolved into an arts centre for the young, creative and environmentally conscious, with galleries and theatres. In the summer, bands make frequent appearances

Bowron Lakes. *7 log cabins | Wells | tel. 250 9 92 88 64 | www.beckerslodge.ca | Moderate*

ECOTOURS-BC LODGE
(145 D2) (*⑳ G12*)
Simple wilderness lodge deep in the hinterland of the Cariboo Mountains, an hour's drive east of Williams Lake. Also 🌐 INSIDER TIP Grizzly bear watching tours, done within nature conservation rules. *6 rooms | Likely | tel. 250 7 90 22 92 | www.ecotours-bc.com | Moderate*

KOKANEE BAY MOTEL ⚜
(145 D3) (*M G12*)

Simple motel overlooking the lake, also log cabins and a camping site right on the shore. *16 rooms | 3728 Hwy. 9 | Lac La Hache | tel. 250 3 96 73 45 | www.koka neebaycariboo.com | Budget*

WELLS HOTEL (145 D1) (*M G11*)
Historic country inn in the gold rush country around Barkerville, with restaurant and bar. *13 rooms | Wells | tel. 250 9 94 34 27 | www.wellshotel.com | Budget–Moderate*

INFORMATION

CARIBOO CHILCOTIN COAST TOURISM ASSOCIATION (145 D2) (*M F12*)
1660 S Broadway | Williams Lake | tel. 250 3 92 50 25, 800 6 63 58 85 | www. landwithoutlimits.com

WHERE TO GO

CHILCOTIN REGION
(144 B–C 1–3) (*M D–F10–12*)
Take a trip into the backcountry on Hwy. 20 if you are at Williams Lake and wish to go deeper into the wilderness. It leads 450 km/280 mi further west through the ranch region of Chilcotin, where forest fires raged in the summer of 2017, and the massive *Tweedsmuir Provincial Park* (campsites, trails) up to the coast at *Bella Coola* – a perfect destination for anglers and wilderness hikers. Not far from here is where Alexander MacKenzie reached the Pacific in 1793 – Canada's first transcontinental crossing. From Bella Coola, a *BC Ferries* boat travels several times a week (reservations are essential).
A good overnight option are the cosy, rustic log cabins of INSIDER TIP *Clearwater Lake Lodge* (7 rooms | Hwy. 20 | Marshall Kleene | tel. 250 4 76 11 50 | www.clear

waterlakelodge.com | Moderate). And there is also the historic 🌐 *Tweedsmuir Park Lodge (Hwy. 20 | Tweedsmuir Park | tel. 604 9 05 49 94 | www.tweedsmuir parklodge.com | Expensive)* with ten luxurious log cabins that is now run as an eco resort.

DAWSON CREEK

(142 B4) (*M 9*) **Dawson Creek (pop. 12,000) would have been an inconspicuous farming village had it not been for *Milestone 0* on the main road in the town centre. This is where the famous *Alaska Highway* begins.**
Now fully paved, the road covers almost 2300 km/1429 mi to Delta Junction, Alaska. Exhibits in the visitor centre in the old station and the *Walter Wright*

⭐ **Mission Hill Winery**
Canada's answer to the wineries of Europe → p. 58

⭐ **Haynes Point Provincial Park**
The most beautiful beaches with the warmest water → p. 59

⭐ **Wildflower meadows on Mount Revelstoke**
A blaze of colour, but only at the height of summer! → p. 60

⭐ **Helmcken Falls**
Spectacular waterfall in the midst of verdant nature → p. 62

⭐ **Fort St James**
Some insights into the lives of the fur traders of yore → p. 64

MARCO POLO HIGHLIGHTS

The Alaska Highway leads to splendid isolation in the Northern Rockies

GLACIER NAT. PARK

(146 C6) (*K15*) **Numerous black bears and grizzlies live in the 520 mi² reserve in the glacier-capped Selkirk Mountains, Hwy. 1 winds for miles through various passes in the park.**

At 1327 m/4354 ft on the *Rogers Pass* a memorial commemorates the completion of the *Trans-Canada Highway* in 1962. You can find valuable tips for hiking routes in the visitor centre next to it – but beware, it often rains along the western flank of the mountains! The exhibits in the visitor centre clearly explain the painstaking construction of the railway 100 years ago. Accommodations and restaurants are in the old railway village of *Golden* (pop. 4100) at the eastern entrance to the park.

SIGHTSEEING & TOURS

GLACIER RAFT COMPANY
Half and full day rafting trips with sturdy rubber boats on the Kicking Horse River. *1509 Lafontaine Rd. | Golden | tel. 250 3 44 65 21 | www.glacierraft.com*

INSIDER TIP NORTHERN LIGHTS WOLF CENTRE
Privately run conservation centre with an enclosure with a pack of grey wolves, which you can view here at close quarters. *Daily in summer 9am–7pm | admission C$12 | 1745 Short Rd. | Golden | www.northernlightswildlife.com*

KICKING HORSE GONDOLA
The ski resort of Golden is not only attractive in winter for skiing. In summer, you can reach the summits by gondola and start hiking tours at the top along

Pioneer Village illustrate the history of the region. The painstaking construction of the highway by American troops in World War II is illustrated in the *Alaska Highway House (Mon–Fri 9am–5pm | admission free | 10201 10th St.).* The *Inn on the Creek (48 rooms | 10600 8th St. | tel. 250 7 82 81 36 | innonthecreek.bc.ca | Budget–Moderate)* is a comfortable motel at the southern entrance to the town.

two fixed rope routes and dine at the highest restaurant in Canada. *Gondola ride C$40 | 1500 Kicking Horse Trail | tel. 800 2 58 76 69*

FOOD & DRINK/ WHERE TO STAY

GOLDENWOOD LODGE ⚜

Located just outside of town, this tranquil retreat is a modern B & B with accommodation in wooden cottages, teepees or in the main lodge. *13 rooms | 2493 Holmes Deakin Rd. | Golden | tel. 250 3 44 76 85 | www.goldenwoodlodge. com | Budget–Moderate*

KICKING HORSE RIVER LODGE ⊛

Environmentally-friendly guest house with geothermic heating in a large log cabin at the edge of the town. Hostel on lower floor. *801 9th St. N | Golden | tel. 250 4 39 11 12 | Budget–Moderate*

HAIDA GWAII (QUEEN CHARLOTTE ISLANDS)

(140 A–B6) (𝄞 B9–11) **'Haida Gwaii', the frequently storm-tossed and rainy archipelago (pop. 6000), formerly the home of the indigenous warlike Haida tribe is now known by its original name and is a genuine 'Galapagos of the North' with its rain forests, sea lions, bald eagles and an incredible abundance of marine creatures.**

The northern *Graham Island* features a well-established infrastructure of roads (and a ferry from Prince Rupert). A large part of the almost uninhabited south-ern *Moresby Island* and its unique ecosystem is now part of the *Gwaii Haanas National Park*.

A very interesting place to visit is the new *Haida Heritage Centre*, where the Haida Native Americans have once again started to carve totem poles and canoes *(daily in summer 9am–6pm | admission C$16 | Skidegate)*.

TOURS

BLUEWATER ADVENTURES

The company offers 5–11 day kayaking trips along the west coast, including the Queen Charlotte Islands. *3252 E 1st St. | North Vancouver | tel. 604 9 80 38 00 | www.bluewateradventures.ca*

LOW BUDGET

A night in the most unusual hostel in Canada costs only C$23 (for members only C$19): the *Shuswap Lake Hostel (229 Trans-Canada Hwy. | Squilax/Chase | tel. 250 6 75 29 77 | www.hihostels.ca)* is in an old general store, and some of the rooms are renovated railway wagons. On request, the Greyhound bus stops right at the hostel.

Even well known ski resorts like Whistler have some affordable restaurants, such as *Ingrid's Village Café (4305 Skier's Approach)*. The little coffee shop right in the pedestrianised zone is popular with the mountain bike and snowboard crowd and serves healthy, reasonably priced food. For C$8 you can tuck into a falafel burger with couscous.

GWAII HAANAS OPERATORS ASS.
Wide range of local providers of guided kayak tours, rented kayaks and boat transport for tours and independent travellers. *Queen Charlotte City | www. placeofwonder.com*

WHERE TO STAY

EAGLES FEAST HOUSE B & B
Four comfortable rooms at the waterside in an old Native American location at the northern end of the island. *2120 Harrison Ave. | Masset | tel. 250 6 26 60 72 | www.eaglesfeast.com | Budget–Moderate*

KAMLOOPS

(145 E4) (∅ 13) Kamloops is the third largest city in the province (pop. 90,000) but not all that impressive by itself. However, since it is located at the crossroads of major highways and features some large shopping malls, this city is a good place to stock up on supplies before starting on a trip into the hinterland.

The centrally located *Victoria Street* has seen a revival in recent years. You will find plenty of shops and restaurants that are definitely worth a visit.

SIGHTSEEING

BC WILDLIFE PARK
Lynx, caribou, cougars and mountain goats: in this park you have a good opportunity to get very close to these rare wild animals of Western Canada – especially as these animals are housed such that it is appropriate to the species. *Daily in summer 9.30am–5pm | entry fee C$15.50 | 9077 Dallas Dr. | www.bcwildlife.org*

FOOD & DRINK

COMMODORE GRAND
This is a brewery pub and entertainment venue for the younger crowd in the old town. It serves good salads, steaks and pizza. Live music starts after 10pm. *369 Victoria St. | tel. 250 8 51 31 00 | Budget–Moderate*

SHOPPING

ABERDEEN MALL
You can shop for hours in this huge shopping mall on the west side of the city. Good shops are *The Bay, Sport Chek* and *Roots Canada. 1320 West Trans-Canada Hwy.*

WHERE TO STAY

PLAZA HOTEL
Historic cattle baron hotel that has been lovingly renovated with lots of attention to detail, in the heart of the city, and with a restaurant. *67 rooms | 405 Victoria St. | tel. 250 3 77 80 75 | www.theplazahotel.ca | Moderate*

RIVERLAND INN
Good, clean motel is nicely situated on the river, well away from Trans-Canada Highway. *58 rooms | 1530 River St. | tel. 250 3 74 15 30 | www.riverlandinn.com | Budget–Moderate*

WHERE TO GO

INSIDER TIP ADAMS RIVER
(145 E3) (∅ G13)
All along the west coast, the salmon swim upstream to spawn and you can experience a spectacular salmon run in early October in the Adams River, about 70 km/43.5 mi north-east of Kamloops. Several hundreds of thousands of bright red sockeye salmon jostle through water

Star studded low tide in the Gwaii Haanas National Park on the Queen Charlotte Islands

that is only knee-deep. Every fourth year is a peak year: within a period of two weeks of more than 2 million salmon come to spawn and die.

LYTTON (145 D4) (*ꟙ G13*)
The tiny village (pop. 400) 150 km/93 mi south-west, at the confluence of the Thompson River and Fraser River, is a INSIDER TIP popular starting point for white water rafting trips. South of the town is the impressive ꟙ gorge where the Fraser River starts on its 100 km/62 mi journey through the Coast Mountains. At *Hell's Gate,* the narrowest part of the gorge, about 50 km/31.1 mi south of Lytton, a ꟙ gondola goes down to the riverbank, where you can watch salmon in the summer fight their way upstream through the whirlpools. *Kumsheen Rafting Adventures (on Hwy. 1 | tel. 250 4 55 22 96 or tel. 800 6 63 66 67 | www.kumsheen.com)* offers rafting on the Thompson and Fraser rivers. A good

place to relax in style for a few days is the ● *Echo Valley Ranch (Jesmond | tel. 250 4 59 23 86 | www.evranch.com | full board | Expensive)* to the north, they also have a Thai spa and horseback riding.

SHUSWAP LAKES (145 F3) (*ꟙ H13*)
The large lake actually has four bodies of water; it is an hour's drive east of Kamloops and is a popular recreation area for water sports enthusiasts. Shuswap Lake itself has a more than 600 miles of deserted and densely forested shoreline. In the small villages such as *Salmon Arm* or *Sicamous* you can rent a houseboat and explore the labyrinth of creeks and coves in peace *(Twin Anchors Houseboat Vacations | 200 Old Town Rd. W | Sicamous | tel. 250 8 36 24 50 | www.twinanchors. com).* Overnight tip for golf fans: the idyllically situated *Inn at the Ninth Hole (6 rooms | 5091 20 Ave. SE | Salmon Arm | tel. 250 8 33 01 85 | www.ninthhole.com | Moderate).*

OKANAGAN VALLEY

(145 F4–5) (⌀ H14) The valley is defined by an elongated chain of lakes, and due to its warm summers and mild climate, it has developed into an orchard and wine area, one that is also a popular recreation and holiday spot. The conditions in the Okanagan Valley are well suited to vineyards: sandy soil, hot, dry summers. Even ice wine (wine from grapes frozen on the vine) does very well here, as winter usually arrives quite abruptly with icy temperatures. Today, there are 120 wineries cultivating grapes in and around the Okanagan Valley. The main varietals include: Zweigelt, Viognier and Pinot Gris, but also Merlot and Cabernet Sauvignon. In some places, such as the Naramatha Bench countryside north of Penticton, there is one winery after the other. Even the Osoyoos tribe in the south of the valley have moved with the times and are now also cultivating vines in their reserve.

The southern end of the valley is extremely dry, even cacti grow there but the slopes around the lakes burst into a blaze of glory in spring, when the apple, cherry and peach trees blossom. In summer and autumn you can buy honey, jam, cider, and of course fresh fruit at roadside stalls.

The wineries that are scattered throughout the whole valley today produce some excellent wines – after more than 40 years of experimentation – and are well worth a visit. On the eastern shore of the approximately 150 km/93 mi long Okanagan Lake is the main town of *Kelowna* (pop. 127,000), where the mild temperatures have attracted many retirees who spend their days playing golf and tennis.

SIGHTSEEING

GRAY MONK CELLARS ↘↙

This is where you can learn all about Canadian wine: hourly guided tours, followed by wine tasting and some spectacular views of the lake. Excellent restaurant ↘↙ *Grapevine* with panoramic view. *Daily in summer 10am–7pm, tours 11am–4pm, otherwise Mon–Sat 11am–5pm | admission free | 12055 Camp Rd. | Lake Country*

MISSION HILL WINERY ★ ●

A magnificent Tuscan-inspired estate high up on the hill that is surrounded by vineyards and orchards. It is the most important winery in the Okanagan Valley. Features a restaurant on the terrace. *Daily in summer 10am–7.30pm, otherwise 10am–6pm | guide C$17 | 1730 Mission Hill Rd. | West Bank | www.missionhillwinery.com*

NK'MIP CELLARS 📀

The ultra-modern winery and cultural centre of the Osoyoos Native Americans features an impressive architecture. Its construction incorporates many sustainable elements of the Native Americans. The centre has a restaurant that serves organic food, a large resort with golf course and a campground. *Daily in summer 9am–8pm, otherwise until 5pm | admission free | guided tours (daily 2pm and 4pm), C$10 | 1400 Rancher Creek Rd. | Osoyoos | www.nkmipcellars.com*

O'KEEFE RANCH

Established in 1867, the cattle ranch was once the largest of British Columbia. Today, it is an open-air museum and its restored ranch house, post office, church and blacksmith provide some vivid insights into the life of the early pioneers. *Daily in summer 10am–6pm | admission C$13.50 | 9 km/5.6 mi north of Vernon on Hwy. 97*

FOOD & DRINK

EARLS ON TOP RESTAURANT

Enjoy fish, steak and pasta on the shores of the lake, with terrace. *211 Bernard Ave. | Kelowna | tel. 250 7 63 27 77 | Moderate*

INSIDER TIP ▶ QUAILS' GATE ESTATE WINERY

Wine shop and elegant terrace restaurant, very nice for lunch. *3303 Boucherie Rd. | West Bank | tel. 250 7 69 44 51 | www.quailsgate.com | Expensive*

SALTY'S BEACH HOUSE 🔆

A popular fish restaurant at the beach. *1000 Lakeshore Dr. | Penticton | tel. 250 493 50 01 | Moderate*

BEACHES

Beautiful beaches, e.g. those in the ⭐ *Haynes Point Provincial Park, are found* in the southern part near *Osoyoos* and in *Penticton.* If you are here at the end of July you can visit the peach festival.

Delicious wines are made here: vineyards of the Mission Hill Winery

MISSION HILL
Family Estate

REVELSTOKE

ELDORADO ☆

Small and stylish hotel overlooking the lake with a restaurant on the veranda. *55 rooms | Pandosy St./Cook Rd. | Kelowna | tel. 250 7 63 75 00 | www. hoteleldoradokelowna.com | Moderate–Expensive*

RIVERSIDE MOTEL

Well-established, comfortable motel close to the shores of the lake, with swimming pool. *45 rooms | 110 Riverside Dr. | Penticton | tel. 250 4 92 26 15 | www.riversidemotel.ca | Budget–Moderate*

SPARKLING HILL RESORT ● ☯

Super luxurious, environmentally friendly hotel that belongs to the Swarovski crystal family. The highlight: the 3.5 million crystals that were incorporated into the spectacular design. There is also the elegant and contemplative *KurSpa* with cold sauna and maple syrup treatments. *149 rooms | 888 Sparkling Place | Vernon | tel. 250 2 75 15 56 | www.sparkling hill.com | Expensive*

WILDHORSE MOUNTAIN RANCH

B & B ranch in an idyllic valley west of Okanagan Lake. Daily horse rides. *7 rooms | 25808 Wildhorse Rd. | Summerland | tel. 250 4 94 05 06 | www. wildhorsemountainranch.com | Budget–Moderate*

THOMPSON OKANAGAN TOURISM ASS.

9912 Hwy. 3 | Osoyoos and 544 Harvey Ave. | Kelowna | tel. 250 8 60 59 99 | www.hellobc.com/Thompson-okanagan. aspx

(145 F3) (*⬦ H13*) **From July to early September the ★ wild flower meadows on Mount Revelstoke, high above the railroad town – an unforgettable sight. About 100 wild flower species grow around the summit.**

In the village (pop. 8500) you will find restaurants, hotels and campsites. Access to Revelstoke National Park is easy: a gravel road leads to the 1938 m/6358 ft high *Mount Revelstoke* (in midsummer a shuttle bus is available). At the summit there are some lovely ☆ short hiking trails while down below in the valley the INSIDER TIP *Giant Cedars Trail* – which leads from the Trans-Canada Highway through dense forests of centuries-old cedars and Douglas fir trees – is also worth a hike.

REVELSTOKE DAM VISITOR CENTRE

The modern visitor centre *(daily in summer 10am–4pm | guides C$6 | info tel. 250 8 14 66 97)* 5 km/3 mi north of the village explains the role of the dam on the Columbia River. Technically minded people can travel 150 km/93 mi further upstream to the mighty *Mica Dam*.

REVELSTOKE RAILWAY MUSEUM

The museum's showpiece is one of the largest steam locomotives to run in Canada. *Daily in summer 9am–5pm, otherwise Thu–Sun 11am–4pm | admission C$10 | 719 Track St.*

GLACIER HOUSE RESORT ☆ ☯

Modern log cabin certified for sustainable tourism. Beautiful views of the mountains, just outside town near the Revelstoke Dam. *26 rooms | 1870 Glacier Lane | tel. 250 8 37 95 94 | www.glacier house.com* | Budget–Moderate

sunny and mild. It lies north of Vancouver and is perfect for a several-day trip to explore its verdant fjord landscape by the Pacific.

No need to wait for a wave: the Skookumchuck Narrows are a playground for kayakers

WHERE TO GO

ARROW LAKES

(145 F4–5) (ⓜ H13–14)
Revelstoke is located at the northern end of the elongated chain of lakes on the Columbia River. On the Highways 23 and 6 you can explore the largely unpopulated region and historic towns like *Kaslo,* hot springs such as INSIDER TIP *Nakusp Hot Springs* and ghost towns like *Sandon*. Car ferries service the towns along the lake shore.

SUNSHINE COAST

(144 C4–5) (ⓜ E13–14) **The Sunshine Coast is protected by a series of small islands and its climate is therefore very**

Hwy. 101 winds 140 km/87 mi along the coastal bays northwards until the road ends in *Lund*. Lining the way are marinas and sleepy fishing villages – today often home to artists and dropouts – and coastal parks such as the *Saltery Bay Provincial Park* (with campsites).

The fishing village of *Egmont* is the start of the impressive 4 km/2.5 mi long hike to the INSIDER TIP *Skookumchuck Narrows* – where the tide forces seawater through the narrows, creating rapids and gigantic whirlpools. Information on the best times: *www.secheltvisitorcentre. com/skookumchuck-narrows*

Guided tours, water taxis and boat trips to the Princess Louisa Inlet and to the Skookumchuck Narrows are offered by *Sunshine Coast Tours (4289 Orca Rd. | Garden Bay | tel. 800 8 70 90 55 | www.sun shinecoasttours.ca)*. Also service for divers and help in finding accommodation.

LUND HOTEL & RV PARK

Heritage hotel that is owned and run by local Native Americans – renovated and right on the harbour. Camping, restaurant and tours organised. *31 rooms | Lund | tel. 604 4 14 04 74 | www.lund hotel.com | Budget–Moderate*

SONORA RESORT ❄ ❀

Luxurious and eco-friendly holiday resort in a dream location on an isolated island. Bear-watching, hiking trails and spa. Accessible by boat or seaplane. *88 rooms| Sonora Island | tel. 604 2 33 04 60 | sonoraresort.com | Expensive*

WEST COAST WILDERNESS LODGE ❄

Well-maintained country inn in a prime location on a cliff overlooking the fjord. *26 rooms | Egmont | tel. 778 2 80 86 10 | www.wcwl.com | Expensive*

WELLS GRAY PROV. PARK

(145 E2–3) *(ᗰ G–H 11–12)* **This provincial park on the northern edge of the Columbia Mountains stretches across an impressive 2000 mi². It is pure and untamed forest wilderness that is particularly well known for its many spectacular waterfalls. Among these are also the 137 m/450 ft high ★ Helmcken Falls, which plunges into a narrow valley.**

Just as spectacular is *Spahats Creek* that tumbles down a 120 m/394 ft deep gorge near the park entrance. Wilderness hikers can explore the reserve on the wide network of hiking trails, and INSIDER TIP the *Clearwater* and *Azure Lake* chain of lakes are ideal for canoe trips.

Dou you like ice and snow? Then make your way to the mountains around Whistler and in the summer visit the glacier

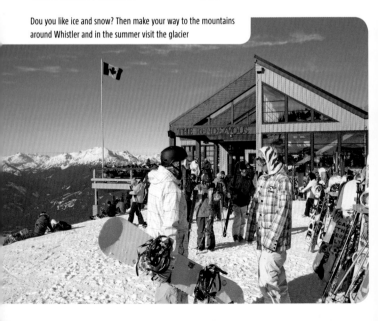

Accommodation and rental services are at the park entrance and in Clearwater. For information and help on planning even more isolated wilderness canoe trips, such as on *Hobson Lake*, contact *Lake Clearwater Lake Tours (Clearwater | tel. 250 6 74 21 21 | www.clearwaterlaketours.com)*.

WHISTLER

(145 D4) (*m F13*) **The well-maintained winter sports resort (pop. 12,000), about two hour's drive north of Vancouver, was the venue for the alpine events of the 2010 Winter Olympics.**
It is hard to believe that this small but by now word-famous town in the snowy *Coast Mountains* was only laid out about 50 years ago. However, with two mountains, *Whistler* and *Blackcomb Mountain*, and nearly 40 ski lifts it is a superlative ski resort. Some of the lifts also operate in the summer, making it easy to walk, bike or go glacier skiing in the summit region. Below in the valley life plays out around the pedestrian zone of *Whistler Village* lined with shops, restaurants and cafés.
The journey to Whistler is in itself worthwhile. The *Sea to Sky Highway* (Hwy. 99), which provides fabulous views across Howe Sound, curves the along the banks of the deep fjords. There are several viewing points, numerous spectacular waterfalls and you can take a cable car ride near Squamish. Information boards are also available that outline the history of the Native Americans in this region.

SIGHTSEEING

AUDAIN ART MUSEUM
The private British Columbian art collection ranges from Native American to modern styles. The museum building only opened in 2016 is also worth a visit. *Wed–Mon 9am–5pm | admission C$18 | 4350 Blackcomb Way*

BC MINING MUSEUM
Old tunnels, jackhammers, panning for gold, and a giant truck are the attractions of this mining museum, which is housed in an old copper mine. *Daily in summer 9am–5.30pm | admission (guided tour) C$30 | on Hwy. 99 at Britannia Beach*

FOOD & DRINK

BEARFOOT BISTRO
This bistro serves fine west coast cuisine: halibut ceviche with melon and chilli, salmon in herb crab butter – and to finish it off wonderful desserts. *4121 Village Green | tel. 604 9 32 34 33 | Moderate–Expensive*

BRASSERIE DES ARTISTES
Popular terrace in the pedestrian area, ideal to sit and people watch. Good breakfast. *4232 Village Stroll | tel. 604 9 32 35 69 | Budget*

STEEP'S GRILL
Restaurant with wonderful views of the Coast Mountains. *At the Whistler Mountain gondola station | tel. 604 9 05 23 79 | Moderate*

WHERE TO STAY

FAIRMONT CHATEAU WHISTLER
This hotel is not only luxurious and elegant, but is also perfectly situated close to the valley ski lifts. Because of the good golf course it is also popular in summer. *539 rooms | Whistler Village | tel. 604 9 38 80 00 | www.fairmont.com | Expensive*

MOUNTAINSIDE LODGE

A modern timeshare facility close to the pedestrian area and the ski lifts. Often cheap deals. *42 rooms | 4417 Sundial Place | tel. 604 9 32 45 11 | www.shellhospitality.com | Budget–Moderate*

INFORMATION

TOURISM WHISTLER

Information centre: *4230 Gateway Dr. | tel. 604 9 35 33 57 | www.whistler.com*

YELLOWHEAD REGION

(140–141 B–F 4–6) (Ⓜ C–G 9–11) **The Yellowhead Highway 16 was opened in 1970 and, apart from the Trans-Canada Highway further to the south, is the second major east-west highway in Western Canada.**

This highway starts in the prairies and runs via Edmonton and Jasper through the isolated north to the Pacific. It follows the old pack route of the fur traders and provides access to the far north of British Columbia (by means of secondary roads such as the Cassiar Highway). The road is named after a blond fur trader whose image is still shown today on the road signs.

SIGHTSEEING

FORT ST JAMES ★ ●
(141 E6) (Ⓜ F10)

The fur trading post, founded by Simon Fraser in 1806, has been restored to an excellent museum village that really brings to life the era of the fur traders, in summer you can even spend the night in the historic *Officer's House* (tel. 250 9 96 71 91 | www.pc.gc.ca/ stjames | Moderate incl. catering). Daily in summer 9am–5pm | admission C$8 | 50 km/31.1 mi north of Vanderhoof on Hwy. 27

'KSAN HISTORICAL VILLAGE
(141 D5) (Ⓜ E9)

An open-air museum village of the Git'ksan tribe, with totem poles and carvings. Dance performances in the summer. *Daily in summer 10am–5pm | admission C$5 | guided tour C$15 | Hazelton*

TOWNS ALONG YELLOWHEAD HIGHWAY

From the border to Alberta, in Jasper National Park, the highway first crosses the dense forests of the Fraser Plateau. West of the logging town (pop. 76,000) of *Prince George (141 F6) (Ⓜ F10–11)* the route then passes through a massive lake district to the Coast Mountains, where the realm of the Northwest Coast Native Americans begins. At *Moricetown Canyon* on the Bulkley River you can watch them fishing salmon in the traditional way during July and August. Nearby, in the *Hazelton (141 D5) (Ⓜ E9)* area are the reserve villages of the Tsimshian tribe, with ancient totem poles that attest to the woodcraft skills of the tribe. Accommodation tip: *Smithers Guest House (5 rooms | 1766 Main St. | Smithers | tel. 250 8 47 48 62 | smithersguesthouse.com | Budget)*, a comfortable B & B within walking distance from the centre of town.

The important fishing, coal and grain port *Prince Rupert* (pop. 15,000) *(140 B6) (Ⓜ C10)* is located at the western end of the *Yellowhead Highway. It* provides access to the ferry system along the west coast: the *BC Ferries* run from here south to Vancouver Island, the ships of *Alaska Marine Highway* run northwards to Alaska.

TOURS

PRINCE RUPERT ADVENTURE TOURS
The company organises half-day boat excursions to watch grizzly bears in the Khuzemateen reservation area. *215 Cow Bay Rd. | Prince Rupert | tel. 250 6 27 91 66 | www.princerupertadventuretours.ca*

INFORMATION

PRINCE GEORGE VISITOR CENTRE
1300 1st Ave., Suite 101 | Prince George | tel. 250 5 62 37 00 | www.tourismpg.com, www.hellobc.com/nbc

WHERE TO GO

STEWART (140 C4) (*Ø D8*)
Take *Cassiar Highway* from Kitwanga for a detour into the mountainous region on the border to Alaska. It is 240 km/149 mi to the town of Stewart at the end of a 145 km/90 mi long fjord. Alaska begins in the pleasantly ratty town of *Hyder* – easily identifiable as

Travel into the past: Fort St James, one of the first trading posts in British Columbia

the bars don't have a curfew. In *Fish Creek* on the outskirts of Hyder, the silver salmon spawn in the summer and you can often see bears and bald eagles as they gorge on the fish.

The ☀ *dirt road* along Fish Creek leads a good 30 km/18.6 mi further up into the mountains with some splendid views of Salmon Glacier.

Comfortable accommodation with a Wild West feel at the [INSIDER TIP] ▶ *Ripley Creek Inn (32 rooms | Stewart | tel. 250 6 36 23 44 | www.ripleycreekinn.com | Budget–Moderate)*. Rooms in lovingly restored historic houses and cabins; the inn also has a good restaurant.

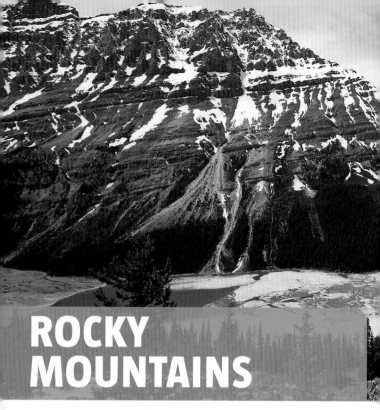

ROCKY MOUNTAINS

Whether from calendar, instagram post or coffee table books, you will know the pictures: emerald glacial lakes, rugged peaks, colourful wild flower meadows and grizzlies feasting on blueberries.

The Rockies region offers all the clichés commonly associated with Canada. It is not surprising then that the mountains on the border between Alberta and British Columbia are also the most famous and most popular tourist region in Western Canada. Five major national parks attract visitors, four of them – Banff, Jasper, Kootenay and Yoho – border on each other and form a nature reserve area that covers 7700 mi². Magnificent mountains at their best – accessible yet unsullied by alpine huts and highways. To date only four passes lead through the

Canadian Rockies and only a few (albeit spectacular) highways access the region. However, the parks have an excellent network of hiking trails. Large numbers of visitors descend onto the areas such as Banff, Jasper and Lake Louise in midsummer. Hotels are usually booked and it can be tough without reservation. You are better off at campsites and at the edge of the parks in places such as Canmore. The Rockies are the easternmost section of the North American Cordillera and Canada. The Rocky Mountains stretch 1200 km/746 mi before ending far north in the Yukon. The mountain range consists of sedimentary rocks, shale, limestone and sandstone, which lay in deposits in a primordial seabed. The mountains were formed 60 million years ago by tectonic

Photo: Peyto Lake in the Banff National Park

The most spectacular road in the world: the Rockies have a network of some of the most scenic national parks in Canada

forces, glaciers then carved out valleys, leaving behind lakes and large moraines – a stunning backdrop for nature lovers and wilderness enthusiasts.

BANFF NAT. PARK

(146 B3–4) (*[map] J12–13*) **The oldest national park in Canada is 2564 mi² of glacier valleys, emerald lakes, dense forests and snow-capped mountains in the Bow River valley.**

In 1885, the Canadian government decided to make the mountain landscape a nature reserve. Due to the strict regulations only a small part of the park was opened to the public, including the town *Banff* (pop. 5000) and some ski areas. A ☆ gondola at the top *Sulphur Mountain* leads to a vantage point overlooking the city and the Bow River. Some hotels were built along *Lake Louise*, but the mountain wilderness stretches around these oases of civilisation, as it has since time imme-morial. Park wardens in the Banff or Lake Louise visitor centres have hiking maps for more than 1300 km/808 mi of trails.

it was built in 1886 by the Canadian Pa-cific Railway. The railway director William Cornelius Van Horne was the driving force behind the construction of this majestic

One of the most spectacular panoramic routes in the world: Icefields Parkway

SIGHTSEEING

BANFF PARK MUSEUM
A log cabin dating from 1903 houses the oldest natural history museum in West-ern Canada, on the banks of the Bow River. *Daily in summer 10am–6pm, other-wise Sat/Sun 11am–5pm | admission C$4 | 91 Banff Ave. | Banff*

CAVE AND BASIN NATIONAL HISTORIC SITE
Exhibitions on the park's history are housed in the old bath house of the hot springs – the park's origin – and all around you will find beautiful nature trails, including the *Marsh Trail (Cave Ave. | Banff)* with its many lookout points.

FAIRMONT BANFF SPRINGS HOTEL ☼
The ostentatious hotel rises out of the for-est at the end of Spray Avenue in Banff;

castle hotel. His belief was, 'If we cannot export the scenery, we must import the tourists', so along with the Canadian Pa-cific Railway (completed in 1885) he also had a series of luxury hotels constructed. The Banff Springs is one of the most beau-tiful examples of these 'railway hotels'.

ICEFIELDS PARKWAY ★
'The most spectacular journey in the world' is the byline of the 230 km/143 mi High-way 93 from Lake Louise to Jasper. The road runs along the ridge of the moun-tains past ancient glaciers and alpine lakes, waterfalls and sweeping summits. It pays to start the journey early, all the best views are to the west, and the morn-ing sun catches the rock walls and ice falls in a soft glow. And keep your cam-era ready, because quite often you will catch the park's animals along the way:

a Wapiti deer or moose, mountain sheep or goats – and with a little luck even a grizzly. Especially in May and June the bears and mountain sheep can be seen in the snow-free valleys. The most beautiful views await at ● � *Bow Summit Pass* viewpoint (2000 m/6562 ft) with the remarkable milky-green of *Peyto Lake* and the canyons further up the valley. Other worthwhile stops include: *Mistaya Canyon*, *Waterfowl Lake* with a beautiful campground and the *Sunwapta Falls.*

LAKE LOUISE ★

Canada's most famous lake shimmers in turquoise at the foot of the 3464 m/11,365 ft high Mount Victoria. On the waterfront at *Chateau Lake Louise* (another railway hotel) is a constant hustle and bustle, but you will find the paths around it much quieter. You will find the trails such as *Big Beehive/Lake Agnes Trail* or the *Plain of Six Glaciers Trail* perfect for a day's excursion. Another perfect location for a selfie is the around 15 km/9.3 mi further south �)̌ *Moraine Lake* in the *Valley of Ten Peaks.*

MOUNT NORQUAY ☀

In winter, the 2133 m/6998 ft high peak above the village of Banff is a very popular ski resort. When you visit in summer, you should take the chairlift and enjoy the panoramic view from the *Cliffhouse Bistro* built in the 1950s and refurbished in 2014. Guided tours for beginners are provided on a well prepared fixed rope route. *Daily 9am–6pm | chairlift C$30 | 2 Mount Norquay Rd. | Banff*

WHYTE MUSEUM OF THE ROCKIES

Topics cover Rockies, the pioneer era and the first Swiss mountain guides. Guided tours to pioneer cabins. *Daily 10am–5pm | admission C$10 | 111 Bear St. | Banff*

FOOD & DRINK

COYOTE'S 🌱

Bistro with creative southwestern cuisine. Also gluten-free dishes and organic ingredients. Open all day. *206 Caribou St. | Banff | tel. 403 7 62 39 63 | Moderate*

★ **Icefields Parkway**
The most spectacular scenic road in the Rockies climbs elevations of over 2000 m/6562 ft → p. 68

★ **Lake Louise**
Despite the crowds of tourists it remains a uniquely beautiful lake → p. 69

★ **Fairmont Jasper Park Lodge**
Luxury in the wilderness – an elegant lakeside lodge → p. 76

★ **Fort Steele**
Perfectly restored gold rush town → p. 78

★ **Kananaskis Country**
The recreation region on the sunny eastern mountain slopes of the Rockies is beautiful and also not crowded → p. 77

★ **Waterton Shoreline Cruises**
Idyllic boat trip, surrounded by mountains, on the US border → p. 79

★ **Takakkaw Falls**
The highest waterfalls in the Rocky Mountains – especially beautiful in the afternoon → p. 81

MARCO POLO HIGHLIGHTS

JUNIPER BISTRO ☼ ⊕
Organic cuisine with regional ingredients and great views over Banff. In newly renovated *Juniper Hotel (Moderate–Expensive)*. *1 Juniper Way | Banff | tel. 403 7 63 62 19 | Moderate–Expensive*

LAKE LOUISE STATION RESTAURANT
Refined regional cuisine in an old Canadian Pacific railway station. *200 Sentinel Rd. | Lake Louise | tel. 403 5 22 26 00 | www.lakelouisestation.com | Moderate–Expensive*

INSIDER TIP ▶ NUM-TI-JAH LODGE
Good place for a break on Icefields Parkway: historic lodge on the shore of Bow Lake. Traditional furnishings and a good restaurant. *Icefields Parkway | 40 km/ 25 mi north of Lake Louise | tel. 403 5 22 21 67 | www.sntj.ca | Budget–Moderate*

SALTLIK
Chic restaurant with a large bar on the ground floor. Serves steaks and fresh fish daily. *221 Bear St. | Banff | tel. 403 7 62 24 67 | Moderate–Expensive*

SUSHI HOUSE
Tiny but excellent, the sushi comes to the table by model train. *304 Caribou St. | Banff | tel. 403 7 62 43 53 | Budget*

WILD BILL'S LEGENDARY SALOON
Hearty Wild West food, live music, lots of wooden decor and plenty of beer make for an excellent atmosphere. ☼ Nice balcony with a view over the action on Banff Avenue. *201 Banff Ave. | Banff | tel. 403 7 62 03 33 | Budget–Moderate*

WILD FLOUR BAKERY ⊕
The bakery not only offers good bread made from organic ingredients but also soups, sandwiches and a good early breakfast for hikers. *Daily 7am–4pm | Banff | 211 Bear St. | tel. 403 7 60 50 74 | Budget*

SHOPPING

Banff Avenue is full of souvenir shops selling T-shirts, fleece jackets and temptations made of chocolate. You will find that the shops in the side streets offer better quality and a greater range of products, such as in the shop INSIDER TIP ▶ *Canada House Gallery (201 Bear St.)* that only sells arts and crafts that were actually produced in Canada.

SPORTS & ACTIVITIES

ADVENTURES UNLIMITED
This is the place where you can arrange for all kinds of active tours in the national

VIRTUAL VIEW OF FIXED-ROPE CLIMBING ROUTES

Would you like to see a view of Bears Hump or a boat trip in Waterton Lakes National Park? Or would you prefer a hike in the Johnston Canyon in Banff National Park? The internet giant Google's technology has also penetrated the Rockies. Nowadays, trekkers are hiking on foot through the hinterland with sophisticated panoramic cameras on their backs, filming numerous hiking trails in the Rocky Mountains, rain forest paths and boat routes in the fjords on the Pacific. This is ideal preparation for your journey: just go to Streetview on Google Maps and you will be amazed how much there is to discover.

parks: be it horseback riding or, if you wish, take guided hiking tours, rafting trips are available too, of course, and in winter you can even do some dog sledding. *211 Bear St. | Banff | tel. 403 7 62 45 54 | www.banffadventures.com*

sion C$7.30 | Mountain Ave. | Banff | www. hotsprings.ca

HIKES

Outside of Banff you'll find some shorter hikes into the *Vermillion Lakes* area,

Fancy a chocolate-covered apple? Sweet fast food on Banff Avenue

BACTRAX BIKE RENTAL

Bike rental for day trips in and around Banff. Good tips for routes. *225 Bear St. | tel. 403 7 62 81 77 | www.snowtips-bactrax.com*

ROCKIES HELI CANADA

Spectacular helicopter excursions over the Central Rockies and the Columbia Icefield. Starts on Hwy. 11 40 km/25 mi east of the Icefields Parkway. *Cline River | Hwy. 11 | tel. 877 5 91 02 22 and 403 8 81 25 00 | www.rockiesheli.com*

UPPER HOT SPRINGS

Relax those muscles after your hike in a steaming bath. *Daily in summer 9am–11pm, otherwise 10am–10pm | admis-*

such as the *Fenland Trail* (just under a mile). Wapiti deer, moose, and beaver are often spotted on the trail despite its proximity to the Trans-Canada Highway. A 2 km/1.2 mi long trail from the parking lot of the Mount Norquay ski area leads to the summit of the ❄ *Stoney Squaw Mountain* with a breathtaking panoramic view over the Banff Valley and *Lake Minnewanka.*

Other great hiking destinations for day trips are: *Spray River valley, Sunshine Meadows* and *Johnstone Canyon.* Also highly recommended: trails that begin at Lake Louise and nearby Moraine Lake, over the *Sentinel Pass* in the *Paradise Valley* or to the *Wenckchemna Pass.*

WHERE TO STAY

Book several months in advance for mid-summer accommodations.

INSIDER TIP ▶ BAKER CREEK CHALETS

Canadian idyll – with well-maintained log cabins and a bubbling brook – in the middle of the park, 15-minutes drive from Lake Louise. *33 rooms | Hwy. 1A | Lake Louise | tel. 403 5 22 37 61 | www. bakercreek.com | Expensive*

BANFF CARIBOU LODGE

Mid/upper range modern hotel. Centrally located in the town. *190 rooms | 521 Banff Ave. | Banff | tel. 403 7 62 58 87 | www. bestofbanff.com | Moderate–Expensive*

ELKHORN LODGE

Simple little motel, well situated in a quiet location close to Banff Avenue. *9 rooms | 124 Spray Ave. | Banff | tel.* *403 7 62 22 99 | www.elkhornbanff.ca | Budget–Moderate*

FAIRMONT LAKE LOUISE ☼

Expensive but the ultimate in a grand setting on Lake Louise. *550 rooms | 111 Lake Louise Dr. | tel. 403 5 22 35 11 | www. fairmont.com/lake-louise | Expensive*

ODENTHAL'S B & B

A simple B & B in a heritage home, with lots of personal attention from the gracious hosts. *2 rooms | 510 Buffalo St. | Banff | tel. 403 7 62 20 81 | odenthal60@gmail.com | Budget*

YWCA HOTEL BANFF

Alternative hostel located in Banff, on the banks of the Bow River. Very cheap 6- and 10-bed dorm rooms and 42 double rooms; kitchen and laundry. *102 Spray Ave. | Banff | tel. 403 7 62 35 60 | ywca banff.ca/hotel | Moderate–Expensive*

A gigantic landscape provides the backdrop to the waterfall Giant Steps in Paradise Valley

BANFF NATIONAL PARK
Visitor centre on Highway 1 in Lake Louise and Banff. *224 Banff Ave. | tel. 403 7 62 15 50 | www.parkscanada.ca, www.bannfflakelouise.com*

WHERE TO GO

KOOTENAY NATIONAL PARK
(146 B4) (*Ⓜ J13*)
The large protected region with an area of 543 mi² around the valley of the Kootenay River is strongly infested by the bark beetle, but the hinterland is good for hiking tours. Various shorter trails lead from Highway 93 (which goes through the park) such as one along the *Marble Canyon* and one to the orange and ochre *Paint Pots* where Native Americans harvested their colours for war paint.

When your muscles are sore from hiking you can relax at the southern entrance to the park where hot water bubbles up (sometimes at hot as 47°C/116°F) at the ● *Radium Hot Springs (admission C$6.40 | www.hotsprings.ca),* the largest (25 m/82 ft) mineral bathing pools in Canada.

A good tip for nature lovers is at the southern edge of the park in the valley of the Kootenay River. The Ⓢ **INSIDER TIP** *Cross River Wilderness Centre (Settlers Rd. | Radium Hot Springs | tel. 403 2 71 32 96 | www.crossriver.ca | Moderate)* has eight cabins and teepees that are solar powered, and all around you will find wonderful hiking areas of far from civilisation.

CROWSNEST PASS

(146 B5) (*Ⓜ K14*) **The Crowsnest Pass is the southernmost pass over the Canadian Rockies. The pass was once an important Native American trade route, today the modern Highway 3 crosses through the densely forested mountains at a height of 1396 m/4580 ft.**

Crowsnest Pass has a series of small towns, such as *Bellevue*, *Frank* and *Coleman,* located along the highway. They were all established around 1900 as mining towns. Frank is infamous for a massive landslide in 1903 that buried the village and killed 60 people. An excellent museum, the *Frank Slide Interpretive Centre (daily in summer 9am–6pm, otherwise 5pm | admission C$13),* shows the history of coal mining in the region, the avalanche and also a trail that winds through the rocks of *Frank Slide.*

JASPER NAT. PARK

WHERE TO STAY

COUNTRY ENCOUNTERS

Very well maintained historic B & B with good restaurant. *9 rooms | 7701 17th Ave. | tel. 403 5 63 52 99 | www.coun tryencounters.com | Budget*

SIERRA WEST CABINS

Very traditional ranch in the foothills of the Rockies with log cabins, saloon, daily horseback riding. Several cattle drives every summer you can participate in. *6 cabins | Hwy. 22 | Lundbreck | tel. 403 6 28 24 31 | sierrawestcabins.com | Moderate*

LOW BUDGET

Admission to Banff or Jasper National Park costs just C$9.80. For a larger round trip the *National Passport* is the cheaper option: C$67.70 per person, C$136.40 for up to seven people in a car – valid for a year for all nine national parks in Alberta and British Columbia.

Youth hostels are rather rare in Canada, but there are about a dozen in prime locations in the Rockies. Some luxurious, some rustic, but all ideal for a bike ride, for instance on the Icefields Parkway. *Around C$26–30 per person, no age restriction, www. hihostels.ca*

Bruno's Bar & Grill (304 Caribou Street) in Banff serves breakfast until late in the afternoon, also good burgers and chunky sandwiches – almost all for only C$10–15. There is also live music in the evenings.

(145 E–F 1–2) *(Ⓜ H–J 11–12)* **Up on the continent's roof: The gleaming white Athabasca Glacier, whose edge is close to the Icefields Parkway, is a highlight of the Rockies.**

The *Parker Ridge Trail* is a short hike that offers more views of the glacier. The 4170 mi² park offers even more: the roaring *Athabasca Falls* on the Icefields Parkway and the idyllic ⚲ *Maligne Lake* or a relaxing soak in the hot springs of *Miette*. Accommodation and restaurants can be found in the only village within the park, *Jasper*.

SIGHTSEEING

ATHABASCA GLACIER

The glacier is part of the 83 mi² *Columbia Icefield,* a remnant from the last ice age, which sends its melt water into three oceans, the Atlantic, Pacific and Arctic. As recently as 100 years ago ice filled the entire valley where Hwy. 93 is today. Signs on the roadside indicate just how fast the glacier is retreating.

The tours offered to the glacier in specially adapted vehicles are more of a tourist trap. However, you can also go on your own or take a guided hike with *Ice Walk (info: visitor centre on Hwy. 93)*. Visit the new ⚲ *Glacier Discovery Skywalk (daily in summer 9am–6pm | admission C$32)* south of Athabasca Glacier and take a stroll on a glass platform 300 m/984 ft above the valley of the Sunwapta River: great views and plenty of thrill included for free.

JASPER SKYTRAM ⚲

Gondola on the ⚲ *Whistler Mountain* offering magnificent panoramic views over the valley of Jasper. There are walking paths around the summit. *Daily in summer 8am–9pm, otherwise 10am–5pm | ticket C$45 | Whistler Rd. | Jasper*

MALIGNE CANYON ☆

Six bridges, steep stairs and an interpretive hiking trail provide access to a spectacular sheer drop gorge on the Maligne River which makes its thunderous way through the rocks. There are routes of different lengths offering fantastic views. Restaurant at the first bridge. *Maligne Lake Rd., circa 12.4 km/20 mi east of Jasper*

on the famous *Spirit Island*. The best time is in the afternoon. *Daily in summer every half hour 8.30am–5.30pm | ticket C$72, reservation in Jasper | 616 Patricia St. | tel. 780 8 52 33 70*

SKYLINE TRAIL RIDES

Half-day horse rides, but also three-day trail rides with overnight stay in a wilderness lodge. Reserve in advance. *tel. 780 8 52 42 15 | www.skylinetrail.com*

HIKES

Find the most beautiful and most popular trails for short hikes at the foot of

The view down from the Glacier Discovery Skywalk is spectacular

TOURS

MALIGNE LAKE BOAT TOURS

One and a half hour cruises on the largest glacier lake in the Rocky Mountains

Mount Edith Cavell and at *Maligne Canyon*. Especially suitable for day hikes and longer trips are the *Tonquin Valley* and the wilderness region to the *Brazeau Lake*.

The mountain goat is the symbol of the Mount Robson Provincial Park

FOOD & DRINK

DOWNSTREAM RESTAURANT
Venison steaks, salmon and bison ribs in a refined atmosphere. *620 Connaught Dr. | Jasper | tel. 780 8 52 94 49 | Moderate–Expensive*

PAPA GEORGE'S
For the big appetite: cosy bar in the Astoria Hotel serving steaks and fish dishes. Serves a very good and big breakfast. *404 Connaught Dr. | Jasper | tel. 780 8 52 22 60 | Moderate*

WHERE TO STAY

ALPINE VILLAGE
Pure nature: here you live in the valley of the Athabasca River in well-maintained and comfortably furnished log cabins: many with their own open fire. *41 rooms | Hwy. 93A East | Jasper | tel. 780 8 52 32 85 | www.alpinevillagejasper.com | Moderate–Expensive*

FAIRMONT JASPER PARK LODGE ★
This is the luxury version of a log cabin in the wilderness: the sophisticated resort hotel is located in a large park on the outskirts of Jasper and overlooks its own private lake. There are rooms in the main building and attractive old log cabins with fireplace. Somewhat busy in high season, otherwise very comfortable and peaceful, also an 18-hole golf course and four tennis courts. *746 rooms | Jasper | tel. 780 8 52 33 01 | www.fairmont.com/jasper | Expensive*

INSIDER TIP TEKARRA LODGE
Rustic log cabins with fireplace, on the outskirts of Jasper. Beautiful riverside location and good restaurant. *42 rooms | Hwy. 93A S | tel. 780 8 52 30 58 | www.tekarralodge.com | Moderate–Expensive*

INFORMATION

JASPER NATIONAL PARK
Information centre opposite the train station on the main road. *Jasper | tel. 780 8 52 62 36 | www.jasper.travel*

WHERE TO GO

MOUNT ROBSON PROV. PARK
(145 E–F2) (*🕮 H12*)
To the west of Jasper is the highest peak in the Canadian Rockies, the

3954 m/12,972 ft summit of Mount Robson. In good weather the mountain is visible from the Hwy 16. Recommended: one to two day hike along the Robson River at the foot of the ice-covered massif. A pleasant overnight option with views of the mountain is ☃ *Mountain River Lodge (4 rooms, 2 cabins | Hwy. 16 | Valemount | tel. 250 5 66 98 99 | www. mtrobson.com | Budget–Moderate).*

KANANASKIS COUNTRY

(146 B3–4) (*꘠ K13*) Banff may be more famous, however, the recreation area of ★ ● Kananaskis Country between Banff and Calgary, on the sunny eastern edge of the Rockies, is just as attractive – and what's best – there are no entrance fees to this park system situated to the west of Calgary and Alberta in the foothills and front ranges of the Canadian Rockies. These canyons show the characteristic of a landscape that was formed by the dissolution of soluble rocks and is common in this region.

Kananaskis Country is noted for recreation and tourism. The majority of the valley is a nature reserve and offers excellent sports activities including a championship golf course as well as a vast network of hiking and cycling paths. The *Peter Lougheed Provincial Park* at the southern end of the valley, where its lakes are framed by 3000 m/9843 ft peaks, is particularly popular. You can enjoy some very good hiking and some fantastic views on the trails around the *Highwood Pass* or on the trail to *Ribbon Falls* and the ☃ **INSIDER TIP** *Mount Indefatigable Trail.*

WHERE TO STAY

DELTA LODGE AT KANANASKIS
Modern, quiet facility in the heart of the region, a good base for golfers and hikers. *412 rooms | Kananaskis Village | tel. 403 5 91 77 11 | deltahotels.marriott. com | Moderate–Expensive*

INSIDER TIP MT. ENGADINE LODGE
Secluded in a high valley this rustic mountain inn is perfectly situated for hikers. Also open in winter. *6 rooms and 3 cabins | Canmore | tel. 403 6 78 40 80 | www.mountengadine.com | incl. full board | Moderate*

WHERE TO GO

COWBOY TRAIL ☃ **(146 B3) (*꘠ K12–13*)**
An hour's drive east of Kananaskis on Hwy. 22, the *Cowboy Trail* is a panoramic

DINING LIKE A TRAPPER?

In a nature loving and wildlife rich country such as Canada one would expect to see more tasty wild duck or juicy moose steak on the menu. Far from it! By law all privately shot game may be consumed privately – wild game for restaurants, however, must come from a farm. So Canadians hunt exclusively for personal consumption and at best you can enjoy wild game by private invitation, but the hunting season is in autumn and by the time the next visitors arrive in the spring the Wapiti will have long since been eaten.

drive that runs through the ranch country at the foothills of the Rockies. Addresses for horseback riding, ranches and restaurants at *www.thecowboytrail.com*. Worth seeing is the *Bar U Ranch*, near *Longview*, a National Historic Site and original 1882 ranch that preserves Alberta's cowboy history. Also horse-drawn carriage rides and exhibitions.

KIMBERLEY

(146 B5) *(∭ J14)* **This town (pop. 6600) on the western edge of the Rocky Mountains is known as the 'Bavarian City of the Rockies'.**

When the local mine closed in 1972 and it seemed that the town would become a ghost town, the city fathers decided to turn their town into a Bavarian village. The mountain scenery is the ideal backdrop and the architecture is now thoroughly alpine. The shops on the *Platzl* pedestrian zone sell Bavarian knickknacks; there is an oversized cuckoo clock and in the restaurants the bands play traditional German music. Even the fire hydrants wear painted *lederhosen* and *dirndl*. The **INSIDER TIP** *Nina's Hillside Garden View* (440 Spokane St. | tel. 250 4 27 46 81 | *Moderate*) serves tasty sandwiches and homemade soup in a garden that has a miniature Swiss village and carvings. At *Kootenay Rockies Tourism (1905 Warren Ave. | tel. 250 4 27 48 38 | www.kootenayrockies.com)* there is information about accommodation, ranches, golf courses and hiking trails in the region.

WHERE TO GO

FORT STEELE ⭐ (146 B5) *(∭ J14)*
About 30 km/18.6 mi east in the valley of the Columbia River the young gold rush era is brought to life in the Fort Steele heritage town. It was founded in 1865 as a post for the North West Mounted

Cafés, small shops and galleries attract many visitors to Baker Street in Nelson

Police and soon became the largest settlement in the region – although it was soon forgotten after the gold rush. Today it lives on as a museum town and more than 60 buildings have been restored or moved here from the surrounding area, costumed actors enact the life of the pioneers, there are heritage livestock displays and a stagecoach *(performances daily in summer 10am–5pm | admission C$17).*

Accommodation is in an old Residential school and mission run by Native Americans, the *St Eugene Resort (125 rooms | 7777 Mission Rd. | Cranbrook | tel. 250 4 20 20 00 | www.steugene.ca | Moderate)* with good golf course and casino.

NELSON (146 A5) (J13)

The oldest town (pop. 10,000) of the Kootenay region is about a 3 hours drive east of Kimberly. It shines with Victorian charm in the neat inner city around *Baker St.* and *Ward St.* The tower-crowned court building, the magnificent bank made of Kootenay marble and the wild west facades of many shops document the elegant past as a rich mining town. Today, thanks to an alternative young scene and the best conditions for mountain biking and hiking in the provincial parks, the town is booming everywhere. Cheap and okay for some nights is the *Mountain Hound Inn* right in the city *(19 rooms | 621 Baker St. | tel. 250 3 52 64 90 | www.mountainhound.com | Budget).*

WATERTON LAKES NAT. PARK

(146 C6) (K14–15) **The 200 mi² park on the edge of the prairies was named after the series of lakes that stretch over the border to the Glacier National Park in Montana, USA.**

Good hiking trails lead into the hinterland which is still completely pristine. A particularly beautiful short hiking trail is the trail to the *Red Rock Canyon*, whose fiery red walls are made up of 1.5 billion year old sediment stone.

At *Cameron Lake* you can hire boats and canoes, and at the northern edge of the park you can observe a small herd of bison in an enclosure. The best views of the lake and mountains is to be had from the terrace of the *Prince of Wales Hotel* at the northern edge of *Waterton Park,* the only village in the reserve.

TOURS

WATERTON SHORELINE CRUISES ★ ●

The company offers boat trips on the *Upper Waterton Lake.* The southernmost point of the cruise is in the *Glacier National Park* in Montana, USA. The views of the majestic mountains are especially good in the early morning. There is also a ferry service for hikers. *Departure from the Waterton marina daily in summer 10am, 1pm, 4pm, 7pm | ticket C$49 | tel. 403 8 59 23 62 | www.watertoncruise.com*

CRYPT LAKE HIKE

The INSIDER TIP most unusual day hike in the Canadian Rockies costs you only C$25 or the price of a ferry ride across Waterton Lake. The trail runs steeply uphill on the other shore. In the end you have to climb up a ladder and through a tunnel to *Crypt Lake* high up in the mountains. *Departures daily in summer 8.30am, 9am and 10am | Waterton Townsite*

NORTHLANDS LODGE

This low-key yet stylishly renovated rustic country lodge, which was built in 1929, is located in the small town of Waterton Lakes, just a 10-minute walk from the Upper Waterton Lakes waterfront and the Waterton Lakes National Park Visitor Centre. *9 rooms | 408 Evergreen Ave. | Waterton Park | tel. 403 8 59 23 53 | www.northlandlodge canada.com | Moderate*

WATERTON LAKES LODGE

Tastefully furnished rooms, some have a fireplace, and there is also an adjacent youth hostel. *80 rooms | 101 Clematis Ave. | Waterton Park | tel. 403 8 59 21 50 | www.watertonlakes lodge.com | Moderate–Expensive*

YOHO NAT. PARK

(146 A–B 3–4) (_ K13_) This park is located in the valleys of the Kicking Horse and Yoho rivers on the western flank of the Rocky Mountains National Park and 'only' 507 mi² in size and not anywhere near as well known as its neighbouring big brother, the Banff National Park.

This fact has its positive sides: it makes it far quieter but no less spectacular, with stunning nature and beautiful mountain scenery including the second highest waterfalls in Canada. You can easily explore the Yoho National Park on a day trip from Lake Louise or Banff or stay in the tiny village of Field.

EMERALD LAKE ☙

The epitome of the Rockies feeling: a surfaced hiking path leads round the shimmering emerald green and turquoise-blue lake surrounding the mountain glacier slopes reaching up to an altitude exceeding 3000 m/9843 ft. A canoe tour is especially great in the summer (can be booked at the lake).

KICKING HORSE PASS

The Trans-Canada Highway traverses the national park and climbs up to the Kicking Horse Pass (1647 m/5404 ft) over the watershed between the Pacific and the Arctic Ocean. To cope with the large differences in height, the railway

CAUTION: BEAR AHEAD!

Chances are you will get your bear photo, for black bears are practically everywhere – you see them curiously snooping around campgrounds and sometimes even leisurely crossing a highway. Grizzly bears and polar bears are a different story altogether: you will encounter grizzly bears only deep in the outback of the Rocky Mountains, and the extremely dangerous and up to 600 kg/1323 lbs. heavy polar bears can be seen only in the High Arctic. Nevertheless, be cautious with black bears too, no matter how cute they may appear: keep a distance when taking pictures, store your food in the evening in the car, and wash your dishes immediately after eating.

The Emerald Lake in Yoho National Park is named after its emerald green colour

engineers drilled two spiral tunnels into the mountain some 100 years ago. If you get lucky, you can watch a curious sight when you see freight trains with more than 100 wagons exiting the upper part of the tunnel while the last wagons are still entering.

TAKAKKAW FALLS ★

The 344 m/1129 ft high Takakkaw Falls fed by melt water from the *Wapta Icefield* provide a magnificent spectacle of nature. The falls are the second highest in Canada, and are around 5 km/3.1 mi north of the icefield. INSIDER TIP In the afternoons the water cascades forcefully into the depths when the noonday sun melts the glacial ice.

WHERE TO STAY

EMERALD LAKE LODGE

The Emerald Lake Lodge is a neat, quiet hotel with a good restaurant. Accommodation is in large log cabins beautifully located on the lake. *85 rooms | Field | tel. 800 6 63 63 36 | www.crmr. com | Expensive*

INSIDER TIP TRUFFLE PIGS LODGE

This modern small lodge is centrally situated but also near the railway line. An excellent ◎ restaurant next door is serving regional organic cuisine. *12 rooms | 100 Centre St. | Field | tel. 250 3 43 63 03 | www.trufflepigs.com | Moderate*

INFORMATION & TOURS

YOHO VISITOR CENTER

Visitor centre with a small museum. Furthermore, there are guided walks several times a week to the fossils of *Burgess Shale,* slate rocks from the Cambrian period. *Hwy. 1 | Field | tel. 250 3 43 67 83 | www.parkscanada.ca, www.burgess-shale.bc.ca*

ALBERTA

The glacier-covered Rocky Mountains are the most spectacular and famous region of the province of Alberta. But one should also not forget the vast remainder of this area, as the Rockies only make up a small part – along the extreme western border – of the 255,200 mi² province.

East of the mountains the endless prairies of Central Canada stretch out into the vast subarctic forest area of the north.

Despite the Rockies tourism, Alberta is above all a land of farmers and ranchers interspersed with small, sleepy villages. However, cowboy and trapper nostalgia does not reign throughout the province. Alberta is also a land of oil workers and high-tech energy companies. In 1914, the first oil well gushed in Turner Valley near Calgary; in 1947 further large oil deposits were discovered near the provincial capital Edmonton. Since then, the two cities – fierce rivals – have boomed, and the oil-rich province provides close to 80 per cent of Canada's fossil energy resources.

The Mesozoic era left the province not only oil and coal: at that time dinosaurs lived in large swamps on the edge of a prehistoric lake and their fossilised bones appear everywhere in the sediment layers of river banks and gullies in southern Alberta. Alberta is the largest dinosaur graveyard in the world – much to the delight of all dinosaur fans.

Land of wheat and forests: buried beneath the wide prairies of Alberta there are both oil treasures and dinosaurs

CALGARY

▨▨ **MAP ON P. 86**
(146 C4) (*Ø K13*) **Skyscrapers, boutiques, sidewalk cafés and urban sculptures – Calgary (pop. 1.5 million) is a thriving metropolis.**

Stroll through the Stephen Avenue Mall. At its eastern end is the revegetated *Olympic Plaza,* created for the Winter Olympic Games 1988. It's like a proud Manhattan in the prairie.

WHERE TO START?
An easy to find starting point is the **Calgary Tower** on 101 9th Ave. Opposite the tower is the Glenbow Museum. The Stephen Avenue Mall is to the north, and the Eau Claire Market on the banks of the Bow River is another seven streets north.

Reason enough for all the extravagance: the oil boom of recent decades rapidly made Calgary the fourth-largest city in Canada.

Calgary's history starts in 1875 when a police post along the Bow River was established to combat illegal whiskey trading. The Trans-Canada Railway was built in 1883, soon after the first ranches were established and Calgary became the Canadian meat industry's capital.The discovery of oil in Turner Val-

CANADA OLYMPIC PARK (0)

The old Olympic centre's *Sports Hall of Fame (daily in summer 10am–5pm, otherwise closed Mon/Tue | admission C$12)* exhibits everything about sport in Canada, including a zip line over the ski jump, free fall, mountain biking trails and bobsleigh rides in summer. *Activities from end June–beginning Oct | ticket C$10–75 | on the western edge of the city | Hwy. 1*

The world's largest rodeo show is attended by around 1.5 million visitors: Calgary Stampede

ley (1914) triggered the first oil boom – and Calgary took off. The city still likes to maintain its cowboy image and for the past century, every July, has hosted the largest rodeo in the world, *Calgary Stampede*.

SIGHTSEEING

CALGARY TOWER ☆ (86 C4) (*j4*)

On a clear day the panoramic view from this 191 m/627 ft tower (with revolving restaurant) is incredible. *Daily in summer 9am–10pm, otherwise until 9pm | admission C$15.50 | 9th Ave. | Centre St.*

GLENBOW MUSEUM (86 C4) (*j4*)

The history of the Native Americans and settlers in Western Canada is documented in three floors of exhibits. *Daily 9am–5pm, Sun noon–5pm, in winter closed on Mon | admission C$16 | 130 9th Ave. SE*

HERITAGE PARK HISTORICAL VILLAGE (0)

The extensive open-air museum on the shores of the Glenmore reservoir depicts life in the Canadian 'Wild West' and features a Native American camp, a fur trader fort an even a reconstructed pioneer village. There is also a steam train and paddle steamer. *Daily in summer 10am–5pm, spring and autumn only Sat/Sun | admission C$26.25 | 1900 heritage Dr. SW*

CITY CENTRE (86 B–C2–5)

Walk from Calgary Tower through the city centre via the pedestrian area at 8th Avenue to the *Devonian Gardens (7th Ave. | 3rd St.)*, a huge tropical indoor garden enclosed in glass at the top of a shopping mall. Just north on Centre Street is the small *Chinatown* and the *Chinese Cultural Centre (197 1st St.)*. East of that, on the banks of the Bow River, are the foundations of the *Fort Calgary* police post, which today houses a visitor centre.

PEACE BRIDGE (0)

An architectural highlight: the Spanish architect Santiago Calatrava built this glazed steel bridge in 2012 for the increasing shuttle traffic of pedestrians and cyclists across the Bow River. Especially attractive in the evening at nightfall, as the bridge is beautifully illuminated. *7th St. SW/1st Ave. SW*

FOOD & DRINK

EAU CLAIRE MARKET (86 B2) *(ω h2)*
Popular restaurants and bars attract visitors in this shopping centre (reconstruction and extension in 2018), e.g. *Bow River Barley Mill*, the hot spot *Joey Tomatoes* and the billiard bar *The Garage*. The historic *1886 Buffalo Cafe* located on the west side of the market is very popular for breakfast.

MODEL MILK (86 B6) *(ω h6)*
Great restaurant in an old dairy. Modern Canadian cuisine is served in tapas-style: bison tatar, halibut or calamari fricassee. *308 17th Ave. SW | tel. 403 2 65 73 43 | Moderate–Expensive*

ORIGINAL JOE'S (86 C4) *(ω j4)*
Small terrace in the pedestrian zone serving delicious burgers, tacos, salads and poutine. Also vegetarian dishes. *109 8th Ave SW | tel. 403 2 62 72 48 | Budget*

THE PALOMINO (86 C3) *(ω j3)*
This is a very rustic BBQ restaurant and bar that serves hearty Tex-Mex cuisine; [INSIDERTIP] in the evening they often have live rock or country music in the basement. *109 7th Ave. SW | tel. 403 5 32 19 11 | Budget–Moderate*

MURRIETA'S (86 C4) *(ω j4)*
This is an excellent steakhouse with traditional wood décor. Also very good fish. *808 1st St. SW | tel. 403 2 69 77 07 | Expensive*

SHOPPING

Western clothes, cowboy boots and Stetsons are without doubt the most

⭐ **Ranchman's Saloon**
Steaks and country music – the Wild West lives on! → p. 87

⭐ **Royal Tyrrell Museum**
Just north of Drumheller, the museum has massive dinosaurs displayed in a primeval landscape → p. 89

⭐ **West Edmonton Mall**
The largest shopping centre in North America → p. 91

⭐ **Head-Smashed-In Buffalo Jump**
Where the Blackfoot tribe drove herds of bison over the cliff → p. 92

MARCO POLO HIGHLIGHTS

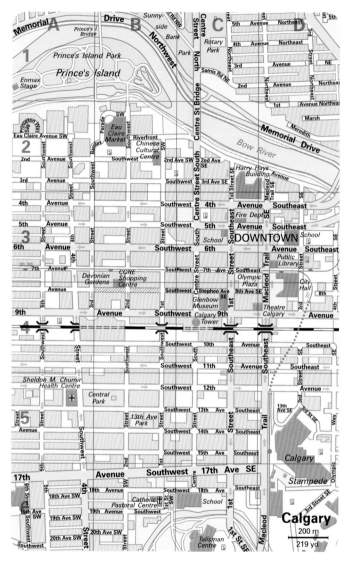

popular souvenirs from Calgary. You will find the best selection at INSIDER TIP *Alberta Boot* (0) *(50 50th Ave. SE)* and *Lammle's Western Wear* in the *Heritage Store (221 8th Ave. SW)* at the *Stephen Avenue Mall*. You will find many more shopping malls along this avenue.

CROSSIRON MILLS ● (0)
Huge shopping centre on the northern edge of Calgary with approximately 200 stores, there are also often discount sales. *Daily 10am–9pm, Sun to 6pm | 261055 Crossiron Blvd., Hwy. 2 north of the airport | www.crossironmills.com*

KENSINGTON VILLAGE (0)
Individual boutiques and galleries, alternative coffeeshops and good pubs: take a stroll through the historically grown district along Kensington Road on the north side of the Bow River and see Calgary at its very best. *www.visitkensington.com*

MEC ● (0)
Everything is sustainable and eco-friendly in this sports shop in the west of the city centre. You will find the most superior equipment ranging from tents to canoe paddles that is essential for a tour in the wilds of Canada. *830 10 Ave. SW | www.mec.ca*

SPORTS & ACTIVITIES

CALGARY MILLENNIUM PARK (0)
The world's largest skatepark is located at the western end of the city centre. Almost 2 acres of pipes, stairs, jumps and ramps that are open to the public around the clock. *1220 9th Ave. SW*

ENTERTAINMENT

Many bars, restaurants and dance clubs are located along 17th Avenue SW between 4th and 8th Street. All country & western music fans should visit the ★ ● *Ranchman's Saloon (0) (9615 Macleod Trail S)*, where – according to the saloon's advertising – all the real cowboys meet (live music; on Wednesdays starting at 7pm INSIDERTIP free two-step and line dancing lessons).

If you don't want to drive very far then you should check out the *Knoxville Tavern (0) (840 9th Ave. SW)* on the outskirts of the city centre. This is a popular music club with country music evenings. Many live music pubs such as the *Night Owl (86 C4) (213 10th Ave. SW)* or the *Cafe Koi (86 B4)*

Shopping under tree sculptures on Stephen Avenue

(🏛 h4) (1011 1st St. SW) that serves Asian-inspired cuisine and features live music are located in the hip quarters on the south side of the city around *11th* and *17th Ave.*

River near the city centre. *19 rooms | 1126 Memorial Dr. NW | tel. 403 2 28 44 42 | www.kensingtonriversideinn. com | Expensive*

A must for dinosaur fans: Royal Tyrrell Museum in Drumheller

WHERE TO STAY

ECONOLODGE (0)
A well-maintained motel that is part of the Econolodge chain of motels. The plus point of this motel: it is conveniently located close to the Trans-Canada Highway. *55 rooms | 2440 16Th Ave. NW | tel. 403 2 89 25 61 | www.econolodgecalgary. com | Budget*

FOUR POINTS SHERATON (0)
Modern hotel near the Olympic Park. *150 rooms | 8220 Bowridge Crescent NW | tel. 403 2 88 44 41 | www.fourpoints calgarywest.com | Moderate*

KENSINGTON RIVERSIDE INN (0)
This is an elegant yet small luxury hotel, which is nicely situated on the Bow

INFORMATION

TOURISM CALGARY (86 B4) (🏛 h4)
Information kiosks, also at the airport and in the Calgary Tower. *238 11th Ave. SW | tel. 800 6 61 16 78, 403 2 63 85 10 | www.visitcalgary.com*

WHERE TO GO

INSIDER TIP ▶ BLACKFOOT CROSSING HISTORICAL PARK ◎
(146 C4) (🏛 K13)
In the middle of the prairies about 130 km/81 mi east of Calgary is the newly built eco-friendly cultural centre of the Blackfoot tribe. The performances and exhibitions include dances, archaeological excavations, and teepee accommodation and guided tours. The location of the

cultural centre also has special meaning: this was where the Prairie Tribes signed the treaty with the Whites that gave up their land in 1877. *Daily in summer 9am–5pm | admission C$10 | Hwy. 842 | Siksika | www.blackfootcrossing.ca*

DRUMHELLER (147 D4) (*ω L13*)

About 140 km/87 mi northeast of Calgary are the *Alberta badlands* – a bizarre barren landscape weathered by erosion – of the Red Deer River. A drive along the 54 km/33.6 mi *Dinosaur Trail* shows multicoloured alluvial fans of deposits and strange rock pillars, where many fossils have already been discovered. The most impressive finds of the dinosaurs that inhabited this region some 65 million years ago are housed in the ★ ● *Royal Tyrrell Museum (daily in summer 9am–9pm, otherwise Tue–Sun 10am–5pm | admission C$18 | www.tyrrellmuseum.com).* The perfectly staged exhibits bring prehistory to life and include well known ones such as Tyrannosaurus Rex through to lesser known ones such as dinosaurs with webbed feet. *www.traveldrumheller.com*

EDMONTON

(146 C2) (*ω K–L11*) From the fur trading era to the gold rush and the oil boom – the provincial capital of Alberta developed from a village to a metropolis of 1.4 million inhabitants.

In addition to the government, the oil industry is the main supplier of jobs. However, there is little sign of the oil industry in the city itself. Its straight streets, neatly laid out in checkerboard style, are lined with manicured neighbourhoods while glass and steel office towers are springing up in the city centre. From a tourist perspective, Edmonton with its international airport is mainly a springboard for trips to the Rockies and – via the Alaska Highway and Mackenzie Highway – to the far north of Canada.

ART GALLERY OF ALBERTA

From the outside clearly recognizable: it's all about art. Over 6000 historical and modern works by Canadian and international artists. *Tue/Wed 11am–8pm, Thu/Fri 11am–6pm, Sat/Sun 10am–5pm | admission C$17 | 2 Sir Winston Churchill Square | www.youraga.ca*

LOW BUDGET

The ● *Banff Centre* is a world-renowned art and music academy, that organizes concerts, exhibitions and events throughout the year, many of which are free or cheaply priced. August features three weeks of jazz with international young talents. *www.banffcentre.ca*

The Edmonton tourist office website offers discounted travel deals for museum entrance fees and special offers: *www.exploreedmonton.com.* You can find also information about the many concerts and festivals hosted by the city. Tickets are available at short notice from *Tix on the Square (9930 102nd Ave. NW).*

Do some advance planning and it will pay off: if you go to British Columbia, you should shop in Alberta. There is no provincial tax, while across the border the tax is 7 per cent. Wine and other alcohol is cheaper in Alberta.

EDMONTON

FORT EDMONTON PARK
The extensive open-air museum depicts the city's history from its fur trading days up to the 20th century. The Hudson Bay Company's fort, built in 1845, has been reconstructed in detail. *Daily in summer 10am–5pm | admission C$35 | 7000 143rd St. | www.fortedmontonpark.ca*

CITY CENTRE
The modern city centre is located on a hill that overlooks the scenic valley of the North Saskatchewan River that is fringed by numerous large parks. All the action is around the vibrant *Sir Winston Churchill Square* with its art galleries and theatres. The main shopping street is the parallel running *Jasper Avenue*.

MUTTART CONSERVATORY
Botanical garden on the riverbank with four futuristic glass pyramids – different ecosystems – make an impressive accent against the urban skyline of the city centre. *Daily 10am–5pm, Thu until 9pm | admission C$12.25 | 9626 96A St.*

ROYAL ALBERTA MUSEUM
New and really gigantic: the largest museum in West Canada will open in the summer of 2018 featuring the history of the pioneers, the culture of the indigenous peoples and the world of the dinosaurs. *Daily 9am–5pm | 9810 103a Ave. NW*

FOOD & DRINK

PACKRAT LOUIE
Chic bistro in the Old Strathcona district with creative new Canadian cuisine and very good pizza. *10335 83 Ave. | tel. 780 4 33 01 23 | packratlouie.com | Expensive*

SABOR
Excellent fish restaurant in the centre of the city featuring Portuguese-Canadian cuisine and a popular bar. *10220 103rd St. | tel. 780 7 57 11 14 | Moderate*

The Art Gallery of Alberta is housed behind a wildly curved facade

SHOPPING

WEST EDMONTON MALL ★
The sixth largest shopping mall in the world is both a shopper's paradise and an attraction. Here you will find more than 800 shops and restaurants, a large amusement park, an artificial lake (with submarines!) and even a wave pool, including a surf wave – all under one roof. *87th Ave./170th St. | www.wem.ca*

ENTERTAINMENT

Night owls will love the university district of *Old Strathcona* on the south bank of the Saskatchewan. Around *82nd Avenue* (called *Whyte Avenue*) are numerous cafés, restaurants and music venues. Country and western music fans should head for *Cook County Saloon (8010 103rd St.)* while jazz lovers will enjoy live bands in the *Yardbird Suite (102nd St./86th Ave.)*.

WHERE TO STAY

FANTASYLAND
A hotel so kitsch you have to see it to believe it: more than 120 of the 355 rooms are styled according to different themes – Arabic, Hollywood, Igloo or Polynesia and so on. *17700 87th Ave. | tel. 780 4 44 30 00 | www.fantasylandhotel.com | Expensive*

ROYAL INN
Comfortable mid range hotel near West Edmonton Mall, with a pleasant bistro. *235 rooms | 10010 178th St. | tel. 888 3 88 39 32 | www.executivehotels. net | Budget–Moderate*

INFORMATION

EDMONTON TOURISM
9797 Jasper Ave. | tel. 780 4 01 76 96 | www.exploreedmonton.com

WHERE TO GO

ELK ISLAND NATIONAL PARK
(146 C2) (*ᐉ L11*)
The fenced 77 mi² park is about 40 km/ 24.9 mi east of Edmonton and provides a protected habitat for a large herd of Plains bison, moose, Wapiti deer and more than 200 species of birds.

JURASSIC FOREST (146 C2) (*ᐉ L11*)
This adventure playground for dinosaur fans of all ages is to be found about 40 km/24.9 mi north of Edmonton: it features true-to-life, moving models of many dino species in a primeval forest. *Daily 9am–7pm | admission C$19 | 2-23210 Township Road 564 | Gibbons | www.jurassicforest.com*

REYNOLDS-ALBERTA MUSEUM
(146 C2) (*ᐉ K–L12*)
About 60 km/37.3 mi south, the museum traces the mechanisation of Alberta's transportation with historical farming equipment, airplanes, cars etc. *Daily 10am–5pm, in winter closed Mon | admission C$14 | Wetaskiwin | history.alberta.ca*

FORT MACLEOD

(146 C5) (*ᐉ K–L14*) **Fertile land on the banks of the Oldman River and the Rockies on the horizon – no wonder that the farming settlement (pop. 3000) was established by the very first settlers in the region.**
As early as 1874 the *Northwest Mounted Police* founded here a fort to curb the whiskey trade with the Native Americans – actually the first outpost in the Wild West.

INSIDER TIP THE FORT MUSEUM OF THE NORTH WEST MOUNTED POLICE

In the (reconstructed) police fort, students perform riding demonstrations in the historical uniforms of the Canadian police. *Daily in summer 9am–6pm, otherwise 9am–5pm | admission C$10–17 | 25th St./3rd Ave | www.nwmpmuseum.com*

HEAD-SMASHED-IN BUFFALO JUMP ★

A name can say it all: this is where the Native Americans drove herds of bison over a cliff. The women waited below the cliff to carve the animals and dry the meat for the winter provisions. The excellent museum nearly 20 km/12.4 mi west of Fort Macleod in the Blackfoot Native American reservation details the lifestyle and hunting methods of the plains tribes. *Daily in summer 9am–6pm, otherwise 10am–5pm | admission C$11 | Hwy. 785 | history.alberta.ca*

FORT MCMURRAY

(143 F3–4) (*ω L9*) **Out in the wilderness of northern Alberta, the city (pop. 70,000) is an oil production hub. It is estimated that there are 27 billion tons of oil in the tar sands below the city.**

In the 1960s an oil plant was opened here in the midst of the endless forest and from this a city boomed. Those interested in technology can visit the state-of-the-art *Oil Sands Discovery Centre (daily in summer 9am–5pm, otherwise Tue–Sun 10am–4pm | admission C$8)*.

LETHBRIDGE

(146 C5) (*ω L14*) **There were wild times in the old days in the today most important town (pop. 100,000) in the south of Alberta.**

In the *Indian Battle Park* on the western edge of the city is the notorious pioneer trading post *Fort Whoop-up,* where American whiskey traders cheated the Native Americans by trading highly overpriced whiskey for their pelts *(May–Sept daily 10am–5pm | admission CS$19)*. Somewhat out of place in the prairie – but very interesting – is the *Nikko Yuko Japanese Gardens* in Henderson Park, a manicured park in the traditional Japanese style *(May–Oct 10am–5pm | admission CS$9)*.

WRITING-ON-STONE PROV. PARK

(147 D6) (*ω L14*) The main attraction of the park in the valley of the Milk River south of Lethbridge, are the hoodoos. These are oddly shaped stone pillars formed by wind and weather. The region was sacred to the Native Americans, and they left behind many petroglyphs. *Guided tours daily in summer | tel. 403 6 47 23 64 to make a reservation*

MEDICINE HAT

(147 D–E5) (*ω M14*) **The largest city in southeastern Alberta (pop. 60,000) depends largely on the natural gas industry, is a major stop on the Trans-Canada Highway, as well as a supply centre for the farms in the surrounding district.**

The hoodoos in the Writing-On-Stone Provincial Park were shaped by the weather

'Medicine Hat' is a very strange sounding name for a town. It probably originated during a time of conflict between the Blackfoot and Cree tribes – a medicine man of the Cree lost his headdress in a battle and his tribesmen interpreted this as a bad omen that actually resulted in a bloody defeat.

WHERE TO GO

CYPRESS HILLS PROV. PARK
(147 E5) (*M14*)

Cypress Hills looms out of the prairies 100 km/62 mi southeast of Medicine Hat – a green oasis in the vast plains. In the ice ages, the region was not covered in glaciers and so the prairie developed its unusual vegetation. In *Loch Leven* you can rent canoes and bicycles. An accommodation tip is the *Historic Reesor Ranch,* an original, century-old ranch just beyond the border with Saskatch-ewan, where guests stay in four B & B rooms and two log cabins *(Walsh | tel. 306 6 62 34 98 | www.reesorranch.com | Budget)*.

DINOSAUR PROV. PARK
(147 D4) (*L13*)

The river bed of the Red Deer River, about 200 km/124 mi north-west, is one of the best dinosaur fossil sites worldwide. 35 species of dinosaur have already been discovered here and Unesco has declared the region a World Heritage Site. There are nature trails and bus tours to the ar-chaeological sites and the visitor centre exhibits a selection of the finds. Fossil enthusiasts who want to stay over will enjoy *Comfort Camping (7 tents | May–Oct tel. 403 3 78 43 44 | albertaparks.ca/dinosaur.aspx | Budget–Moderate)* on the banks of the Red Deer River, where all the equipment – including proper beds – is included.

NORTHERN CANADA

For wilderness enthusiasts and nature lovers, the region north of the 60th latitude is the most spectacular part of Canada. It is a raw, largely untouched land, whose austere beauty provides ample material for tales of trappers, prospectors and lost expeditions.

The massive northern region comprises about a third of Canada's total area. Politically, the north is divided into three territories: the mountainous Yukon in the west (which experienced the largest gold rush of all time about 100 years ago in the Klondike), the Northwest Territories around the huge Mackenzie River Valley and the Great Slave Lake and the Nunavut Territory (established in 1999) extending from Hudson Bay to the North Pole. Only about 36,000 people live in the Yukon, 80,000 in the Northwest Territories and Nunavut is predominantly inhabited and governed by the Inuit. The Northwest Territories are home to the Dene Native Americans who are now also demanding their own, independent region. Good equipment and careful planning are essential for a trip into Northern Canada, even in a nice and warm summer (30°C/86°F). Travel is easiest around the Great Slave Lake and in the Yukon, which have roads and a tourist infrastructure. The most important routes in the north are the Alaska Highway and the Mackenzie Highway from Edmonton to Yellowknife on the Great Slave Lake. The roads from there into the hinterland are only gravel tracks: the Liard Highway to the Nahanni National Park, the Klondike

Photo: Dog sleds on frozen Lake Laberge

In the footsteps of Jack London: on the backcountry roads of the far north you will often not see another soul for hours

Highway to the historic gold rush area – brought to life by the stories of Jack London – around Dawson City. All the other Arctic regions can only be reached by aircraft.

DAWSON CITY

(138 A–B2) (*m B1*) ★ ● **The gold rush era lives on in this practically deserted ghost town that was known in the 1900s as the 'Paris of the North'.**

About 30,000 people lived here during the *Klondike Gold Rush* in the 1900s, and the town at the mouth of the Klondike River in the Yukon is now a Historic Site characterised by Wild West sidewalks and wooden facades. There are only around 2000 inhabitants in Dawson City today; their income is mainly from tourism, but the current high price of gold has once again drawn miners to the surrounding goldfields. For the most beautiful views follow the gravel road up to the 1000 m/3281 ft high lookout point ☆ *Midnight Dome*.

SIGHTSEEING

DAWSON CITY MUSEUM

The museum depicts the gold rush era with old photos, mining equipment and tools, film showings and

the historic paddle steamer, the *SS Keno* on the Yukon River.

FOOD & DRINK

KLONDIKE KATE'S

Cosy pub in historic building with a terrace. Great steaks and brunch on Sundays. Cabins are rented too. *3rd Ave./ King St. | tel. 867 9 93 65 27 | Moderate*

Today, only a few gold diggers come to Dawson City, but lots of tourists

gold panning demos. *Daily in summer 10am–6pm | admission C$9 | 5th Ave./ Church St.*

HISTORIC DISTRICT

Cancan girls dance in *Diamond Tooth Gertie's Gambling Hall,* the *Palace Grand Theatre* performs dramas, while photos, documents and letters in *Jack London's Cabin* bring his novels to life. Many of the renovated old buildings are open to the public, such as the old *post office (King Street)*, the elegant *Commissioner's Residence (guides | Front Street)*, as well as

WHERE TO STAY

BOMBAY PEGGY'S

The former brothel is now a comfortable guest house. They also have INSIDER TIP a good pub though. *9 rooms | Princess St./2nd Ave. | Phone 867 9 93 69 69 | www.bombaypeggys.com | Moderate*

ELDORADO

52 modern and comfortable rooms. With a restaurant and a saloon. *3rd Ave./Princess St. | tel. 867 9 93 54 51 | www.eldoradohotel.ca | Moderate*

INFORMATION

VISITOR RECEPTION CENTRE

The visitor centre also organises slide shows and guided tours of the city. *1102 Front St./King St. | tel. 867 9 93 55 66 | www.dawsoncity.ca*

WHERE TO GO

BONANZA CREEK (138 B2) (*山 B1*)

The first gold was discovered in 1896 5 km/ 3.1 mi south in the Klondike River valley. Two historic sites, a mining claim and a preserved sluice dredge, *Dredge No. 4,* testify to the rigors of the gold miners.

DEMPSTER HIGHWAY ★ ●
(138 B1–2) (*山 B–C1*)

This gravel road runs over 700 km/ 435 mi from Dawson City to the deserted tundra regions north of the Arctic Circle to the Inuit settlement of *Inuvik* in the Mackenzie Delta and since 2017 onwards to the polar sea at Tuktoyaktuk. There are only two tiny Native American villages and a petrol station along the entire route; otherwise there is nothing but the Arctic wilderness. The highway is especially scenic in early September when autumn transforms the foliage into a sea of colour.

TOP OF THE WORLD HIGHWAY/TAYLOR
HIGHWAY ☀ (138 A2) (*山 A–B1*)

The most scenic stretch is the 270 km/ 168 mi section from the Yukon to Alaska – a panoramic ride through isolated mountain peaks, verdant valleys and old gold mining areas. There is only one place to stop along the way, the old mining hamlet of *Chicken* in Alaska. At *Tok* Highway 9 connects to the Alaska Highway, making a round trip back to Whitehorse possible. *(Road only open from late May–Sept)*

HAINES JUNCTION

(138 B5) (*山 B4*) The tiny, hill-fringed village where the Alaska Highway meets the Haines Highway is a good starting point for trips to the Kluane National Park. The park covers 8495 mi² of pristine mountain wilderness in the westernmost corner of the Yukon.

Canada's highest peak, *Mount Logan,* is in the ice-covered St Elias Mountains on the border to Alaska. The Alaska Highway runs along the northern edge of the park (visitor centre in Haines Junction) on the banks of the 150 mi² *Kluane Lake* where trails lead to the foothills of the *Kluane Range*. The east of the park holds *Kathleen Lake,* a beautiful hiking region. The ☀ *Kluane B & B (8 rooms | Alaska Hwy., 55 km/34.2 mi west of*

★ **Dawson City**
The gold rush city in the Klondike is still a bustling little town → p. 95

★ **Dempster Highway**
The famed wilderness road runs from Dawson City up into the Mackenzie Delta → p. 97

★ **S.S. Klondike**
An original paddle steamer from the good old gold rush days of yore → p. 99

★ **Prince of Wales Northern Heritage Centre**
Preserving pioneer history and indigenous cultures → p. 101

MARCO POLO HIGHLIGHTS

Haines Junction | tel. 867 841 42 50 | www.kluanecabins.com | Budget) offers rustic cabins, great breakfasts and a spectacular location. Excursions by plane over icy mountains and overnight stays in a glacier camp up in the *St Elias Mountains* can be booked at *Icefield Discovery (from C$250 | tel. 867 8 41 42 04 | www.icefielddiscovery.com).*

INUVIK

(0) (*Ⅲ 0*) About 3000 people (Inuit, Dene and other cultures) live here on the eastern edge of the vast Mackenzie

LOW BUDGET

On the quiet western side of the Yukon River is the northernmost hostel in Canada, the *Dawson City River Hostel (Dawson City | tel. 867 9 93 68 23 | www.yukonhostels.com).* Accommodation costs C$14–22 and is in simple log cabins or on the campsites. Only open in the summer.

Alternative tourists, motor home travellers and locals – they all meet at the ✪ *Alpine Bakery (411 Alexander St. | tel. 867 6 68 68 71 | www.alpinebakery.ca)* in Whitehorse where you can get very reasonably priced *caffè latte*, healthy muffins and organic bread.

For only C$6.30 you can relive the gold rush era: the bard Robert Service, played by an actor, recites works such as 'The Spell of the Yukon' twice a day. Very atmospheric. *Robert Service Cabin | ask for times at the Visitor Centre | 8th Ave. | Dawson City*

Delta and the town lives up to its name of 'Place of the People'.
After the 700 km/435 mi long ride on the *Dempster Highway* from Dawson City, you deserve a few sightseeing flights over the area, such as to the remote trapper village of *Aklavik* in the middle of the 80 km/49.7 mi wide river delta, to the old whaling station on *Herschel Island*, or to the Inuit settlement of *Tuktoyaktuk* on the Arctic Ocean coast. Trips such as these can be organised by, for example, *Tundra North (tel. 800 4 20 96 52 | www.tundranorthtours.com),* who offer guided tours to the Arctic Ocean on the new Tuk Highway.

WATSON LAKE

(139 F5) (*Ⅲ E5*) Since the construction of the Alaska Highway in 1942 the village (pop. 800) in the southern Yukon has become an important supply base.
It is also home to the *Watson Lake Signpost Forest,* with 80,000 signposts from all over the world, started 75 years ago by a homesick soldier. Next to it is a modern *Interpretive Centre* that details the history of the Alaska Highway.

WHERE TO GO

MUNCHO LAKE (141 E1) (*Ⅲ F6*)
The 11 km/6.8 mi long emerald green lake lies about 300 km/186 mi southeast on the Alaska Highway (in British Columbia). Stop off at the *Liard River Hot Springs Park* and soak away the dust of the wilderness.
The **INSIDER TIP** ▶ *Northern Rockies Lodge (45 rooms, 10 cabins | Mile 462 | tel. 250 7 76 34 81 | www.northernrockies*

lodge.com | *Moderate*) offers rooms and air safaris into the Nahanni National Park.

NAHANNI NAT. PARK
(139 E–F 3–4) (*⃞ F–G 4–5*)

The park is an hour's flight northeast of Watson Lake and is a popular white water rafting destination: the *South Nahanni River* runs through the *Mackenzie Mountains* before thundering over the 90 m/295.3 ft high *Virginia Falls* and

through the hazardous *Miles Canyon*, on their way to the gold fields of the Klondike. You can learn more about its golden era in the *MacBride Museum* and in the *Old Log Church Museum*.

SIGHTSEEING

S.S. KLONDIKE ★

Built in 1937, the historic paddle steamer has been lovingly restored and is now open to the public. Today it can be visited

Seven months of winter in Yukon: where a real fur collar is no luxury

into deep gorges. In Whitehorse companies such as *Nahanni River Adventures* (tel. 867 6 68 31 80 | www.nahanni.com) offer guided canoe trips and wilderness expeditions.

WHITEHORSE

(138 C5) (*⃞ C4*)
Yukon's capital (pop. 25,000) stretches out along the broad bank of the Yukon River. Its first period of prosperity was around 1900.
Thousands of prospectors arrived at that time on crudely built rafts and boats

in a dry dock on the banks of the Yukon River. *Daily in summer 9.30am–5pm | admission C$6 | 2nd Ave.*

TOURS

A good resource is the *Wilderness Tourism Association* website that lists more than 20 adventure companies: *www.yukonwild.com*.

KANOE PEOPLE ●

Here you will get all the equipment for a leisurely canoe trip on the Yukon to Dawson City including canoes, tents and all the other things you will need on the trip. Guided tours are also offered. *1147 1st Ave. | tel. 867 6 68 48 99 | www.kanoe people.com*

FOOD & DRINK

DIRTY NORTHERN PUBLIC HOUSE
Popular pub with very good pizza and regional beer, in the evening often live bands. *103 Main St. | tel. 867 633 3305 | Budget*

KLONDIKE RIB & SALMON BBQ
Rustic restaurant in an old pioneer cabin; good chowder, salmon and bison steaks. *2116 2nd Ave. | tel. 867 6 67 75 54 | Expensive*

WHERE TO STAY

HIGH COUNTRY INN
Centrally located with a very popular INSIDER TIP terrace bar and BBQ grill: *The Deck. 82 rooms | 4051 4th Ave. | tel. 867 6 67 44 71 | www.highcountryinn. yk.ca | Moderate*

HISTORICAL GUEST HOUSE
Cosy, simple accommodation, in the city centre with a very helpful host. *3 rooms | 5128 5th Ave. | tel. 867 6 68 39 07 | www. historicalguesthouse.com | Budget–Moderate*

INN ON THE LAKE
An idyllic cabin style lodge in a quiet location on Marsh Lake with superb cuisine. *8 rooms | Alaska Hwy. 35mins drive from Whitehorse | tel. 867 6 60 52 53 | www.innonthelake.com | Moderate–Expensive*

TAGISH WILDERNESS LODGE ⊙
This is a block-house lodge that is run by a Swiss family on a secluded lake; it is only accessible by boat or seaplane. *4 cabins | Tagish | tel. 867 3 32 21 13 | www.tagishresort.com | Expensive (only full board)*

INFORMATION

TOURISM YUKON
Hanson St./2nd Ave. | Whitehorse | tel. 800 6 61 04 94 | www.travelyukon.com

WHERE TO GO

INSIDER TIP **ATLIN** ⬧ (139 D6) (*ப C5*)
Its magnificent location, surrounded by mountains on the shores of Atlin Lake, makes the trip to Atlin and the roughly 170 km/106 mi drive south well worth it. The picturesque and weathered gold mining village (it was founded in 1898 during the Klondike gold rush) is actually located in British Columbia but it can be accessed only from the Yukon. Today, around 500 people live in and around Atlin: gold prospectors, artists, dropouts. One thing you must do is to take a scenic flight over the glacier-covered Coast Mountains with *Atlin Air Charters (tel. 250 6 51 00 25)*. Tip for overnight stays: *Glacier View Cabins (tel. 250 6 51 76 91 | www.glacierviewcabins.ca | Budget–Moderate)* – three cabins with a great view. The Swiss owners also organise guided canoe tours.

YELLOWKNIFE

(0) (*ப K4*) **You have the best views over the modern capital of the Northwest Territories from** ⬧ *Pilot's Monument* **on a bare brow of a hill.**

There are about 19,000 inhabitants and they are either state employees or involved in the two gold mines. Around 1990, diamonds were also discovered here which are now prospected in large open-cast mines.

SIGHTSEEING

PRINCE OF WALES NORTHERN HERITAGE CENTRE ★

The best museum in the Northwest Territories. It has exhibits about the flora and fauna of the Arctic and Yellowknife is a great place to see the northern lights. *Daily in summer 10.30am–5pm | admission free | Frame Lake St./48th St.*

FOOD & DRINK/ WHERE TO STAY

BAYSIDE B & B ☆☆

Large wooden house on Great Slave Lake, with a popular restaurant. *5 rooms | 3505 McDonald Dr. | tel. 867 4 45 50 03 | www. baysidenorth.com | Budget–Moderate*

THE WILDCAT CAFÉ

An institution: hearty pioneer cuisine and caribou steaks. *3904 Wylie Rd. | tel. 867 8 73 40 04 | Moderate*

INFORMATION

NORTHWEST TERRITORIES TOURISM

Visitor centres at the airport and in the Prince of Wales Centre | Yellowknife | tel. 867 8 73 72 00 | www.spectacular nwt.com

WHERE TO GO

WOOD BUFFALO NAT. PARK
(143 D–E 1–2) *(ᗕ L8)*

The 17,500 mi² reserve in the delta of the Peace and Athabasca rivers is the largest national park in Canada. The park was established in 1922 to protect the world's largest herd of free roaming wood bison. The endless forests are home to 6000 wild bison while the wetlands are home to numerous water birds, including rare cranes and the longest bird native to North America, the American white pelican.

Some gravel tracks lead from *Fort Smith* (visitor centre) into the reserve. You can also take a cruise on the Slave River.

The Wood Buffalo National Park is home to some 6000 animals

DISCOVERY TOURS

① WESTERN CANADA AT A GLANCE

START: ① Calgary
END: ⑲ Vancouver

Distance:
➡ 2500 km/1553 mi

14 days
Driving time
(without stops)
35 hours

COSTS: C$300 for gas (car), C$40 canoe rental at ⑪ Emerald Lake in Yoho National Park, C$150 rafting tour at ⑯ Lytton, C$37 ride with ⑱ Sea-to-Sky Gondola in Squamish

WHAT TO PACK: Hiking boots, rain/wind jacket and sweater, do not forget sun protection and mosquito repellent in summer

IMPORTANT TIPS: Bears are frequently seen especially in early summer – keep distance and leave no food around! Tip: You sometimes can save the car transfer fee if you follow the route in west-east direction.

Would you like to explore the places that are unique to this region? Then the Discovery Tours are just the thing for you – they include terrific tips for stops worth making, breathtaking places to visit, selected restaurants and fun activities. It's even easier with the Touring App: download the tour with map and route to your smartphone using the QR Code on pages 2/3 or from the website address in the footer below – and you'll never get lost again even when you're offline.

TOURING APP

→ p. 2/3

An introductory tour, ideal for first-timers: the route from the prairies in Calgary to the ice-covered peaks of the Rockies, on to the lake districts of British Columbia and the Pacific coast in Vancouver, show the many facets of Western Canada. There is ample time for hiking and experiencing nature along the route and other tours are easy to combine. Best travel time: June to September.

A day to get settled in **① Calgary** → p. 83: stroll in **Stephen Avenue Mall**, visit **Heritage Park** and shop cheap, as there is no provincial tax in Alberta. Benefit from the great bargains for clothes and shoes the next morning.

DAY 1

① Calgary

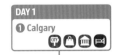

Photo: View from Sulphur Mountain in Banff National Park

103

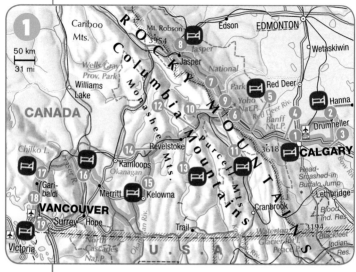

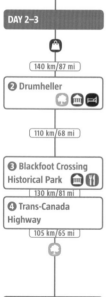

DAY 2–3

🛍️

140 km/87 mi

② Drumheller
🛍️ 🏛️ 🛏️

110 km/68 mi

③ Blackfoot Crossing
Historical Park 🏛️ 🍴

130 km/81 mi

④ Trans-Canada
Highway

105 km/65 mi

🛍️

DAY 4–5

⑤ Banff National Park
🛍️ 🚶 🛏️

240 km/149 mi

Right at the **exit from Calgary at the north end of the City at Crossiron Mills** *(Hwy. 2, Exit 273)* is a huge discount mall you might get lost in. Now its time to **head east on Hwys. 567 and 9 and into the wide plains, where you get to ② Drumheller → p. 89** and the spectacular dinosaur finds in the Valley of the Red Deer River. Do you fancy some historic excavations of your own? The helpful guides of the great **Royal Tyrrell Museum → p. 89** offer half-day excursions that are exciting not just for small children – they are exciting for young and old. The next day, when you are **on the way back, take Hwys. 56 and 1**; it is well worth to stop for the exhibition of the ③ **Blackfoot Crossing Historical Park → p. 88** – and for a bison burger in the Café of the Native American Museum. **Head westwards on the way back via Calgary: the ④ Trans-Canada Highway runs along Bow River** from the plains to the Rocky Mountains, crossing the old tribal land of the .Blackfoot Native Americans. Soon you'll see the snowy peaks of the Rockies on the horizon. **The mountains get closer to Hwy. 1 near Canmore** and get higher and higher.

Directly behind the first sign that warns of bears is the **entrance to the ⑤ Banff National Park → p. 67** – this is the oldest and most famous conservation area in the Rocky Mountains. You should plan to stay for two nights in **Banff** to have time for some hiking in the mountains – at the **Vermilion Lakes** right at the outskirts of Banff or near **Lake Louise**, **Moraine Lake** and **Johnston**. The panoramic bar and terrace of the historic **Banff Springs Hotel** that overlooks the valley of the Bow River is perfect for an evening drink.

The next leg of your route covers the most beautiful panoramic road in the Rocky Mountains, the ⑥ **Icefields Parkway** → p. 68. It is a splendidly constructed route that runs parallel to the mountain ridges to the north. Definitely keep your camera ready, as you will get some spectacular views. Especially beautiful: the narrow gorge of the **Mistaya River** and the spectacular panoramic views at **Waterfowl Lake**. Follow the steep climb to the 2035 m/6677 ft high **Sunwapta Pass** and, if the weather is good, take a two-hour walk on the ⑦ INSIDERTIP **Parker Ridge Trail** before the route leads by the **Athabasca Glacier** → p. 74 to ⑧ **Jasper National Park** → p. 74. You should stop for another day: hike in the **Maligne Canyon** → p. 75, take a gondola ride to the summit above the city and a boat cruise on **Maligne Lake**.

Back to the south: you will be amazed how different the mountains look when you are on the trip back. This is why you should get up early for the **return trip on Icefields Parkway**. If you are lucky and it's sunny, the sun will light up the peaks in an early alpenglow, and quite often you can observe bears and mountain sheep along the road. At lunchtime, stop at the trapper lodge ⑨ **Num-Ti-Jah** → p. 70 on Bow Lake. **From Lake Louise, follow Hwy. 1 westwards across the ridge of the Rockies to British Columbia** (1 hour time difference) and into the ⑩ **Yoho National Park** → p. 80, where the highest waterfalls in the Rocky Mountains, the **Takakkaw Falls** → p. 81, shoot from the Waputik Icefield in an impressive arch. Treat yourself to a canoe trip on or a walk around the idyllic ⑪ **Emerald Lake** before stopping at **Field** for the night, e.g. at the **Truffle Pigs Lodge** → p. 81 with a very good restaurant. You will find more good motels and B & Bs in Golden.

Head westwards on the Trans-Canada Highway: travel via Golden (attention: time zone: −1 h), through the jagged mountain range of the Columbia Mountains in ⑫ **Glacier National Park** → p. 54. **It is immediately followed by the smaller** ⑬ **Revelstoke National Park** → p. 60. If you

DAY 6–7
⑥ Icefields Parkway

65 km/40.4 mi

⑦ Parker Ridge Trail

115 km/71 mi

⑧ Jasper National Park

DAY 8

325 km/202 mi

⑨ Num-Ti-Jah

65 km/40.4 mi

⑩ Yoho National Park

30 km/18.6 mi

⑪ Emerald Lake

175 km/47 mi

DAY 9–10
⑫ Glacier National Park

45 km/28 mi

⑬ Revelstoke National Park

95 km/59 mi

⑭ Sicamous

100 km/62 mi

⑮ Okanagan Valley

DAY 11–14

400 km/249 mi

⑯ Lytton

190 km/118 mi

⑰ Whistler

62 km/38.5 mi

⑱ Sea-to-Sky Gondola

60 km/37.3 mi

⑲ Vancouver

take this route in midsummer, you should take a trip to the flower fields and the magnificent trails near the summits. After you've stayed a night in **Revelstoke**, you must pass a last and densely forested mountain range, the **Monashee Mountains**. Deep in the forests is a place called **Craigella-chie**. It is a very historic train station and was the location where the final nail of the Trans Canada Railway line was hammered in on November 9, 1885. **Shortly afterwards, in ⑭ Sicamous**, it definitely would count as a sin if you missed the **Dutchman Dairy** *(1321 Maier Rd. | tel. 250 8 36 43 04)* – those giant ice cream scoops do taste phenomenally good. **In Sicamous, the route branches off from Hwy. 1 to the south** and into a valley that has everything to do with wine, it's the **⑮ Okanagan Valley → p. 58**. Those numerous wineries along Hwy. 97 around the towns of Kelowna and Penticton make amazingly fine wine. It's pleasure time now: tastings in wineries, followed by delicious lunches in terrace bars and extensive swimming in warm lakes. Tip: **take the Boucherie Road west of the town Kelowna on the western shore of the Okanagan Lake** to the wineries such as **Quails' Gate** and **Mission Hill Winery → p. 58**. To end the day, take your time and enjoy an evening stroll along the bustling beach promenade in **Penticton**.

The ranchland of British Columbia comes after Penticton: It is dry like a desert and, like the desert, it's almost always sunny. **The route will now wind along the Hwys. 5A, 8 and 1** northwards through rolling hills and large cattle pastures to the Fraser River Canyon. In a hot summer you should go rafting at **⑯ Lytton → p. 57**. **Hyak Rafting** *(C$180| tel. 600 7 34 86 22 | www.hyak.com)*, which offers an afternoon tour that should be perfect for your timing. **Hwy. 99 climbs from the river across the sparsely populated Coast Mountains westwards and leads to ⑰ Whistler → p. 63**, the alpine venue of the Olympic Winter Games of 2010. Time for a ride to Whistler Mountain, a bike or zip line tour or a round of golf. Continue the next morning and at Squamish you'll see the first arm of the sea, the **Howe Sound**. You get an even better view from the **⑱ Sea-to-Sky Gondola** *(36800 Hwy. 99 | tel. 604 8 92 25 50)*, which takes you 885 m/2904 ft above the fjord in ten minutes. At the top await trails, a spectacular rope bridge and a restaurant. It's only an hour's drive full of beautiful panoramas **on Hwy. 99 to the destination ⑲ Vancouver → p. 32**, where you should plan another day for sightseeing.

2 HEADING SOUTH: FORESTS AND TRANQUIL LAKES

START: ❶ Vancouver
END: ❶❺ Calgary

10 days
Driving time
(without stops)
28 hours

Distance:
➡ 1900 km/1180 mi

COSTS: C$200 for petrol (car)
WHAT TO PACK: Hiking boots, sunscreen and bathing suit

IMPORTANT TIPS: The beaches in the ❻ Okanagan Valley are well attended during midsummer. The forest lakes in the hinterland are much more quiet and nicer – but also colder.

The sunny south of the provinces is ideal for nature lovers and families that wish to enjoy a peaceful holiday in Wild West corners, museum villages and wineries, in ghost towns from the gold rush era and in national parks like Waterton Lakes.

The route starts in ❶ Vancouver → p. 32 and leads **on the Trans-Canada Highway eastward through the fertile Fraser Valley.** A good prelude to the journey into the pioneering country: the museum village ❷ Fort Langley → p. 39, which revives the days of the fur traders. A spectacular short hike in ❸ Hope is the INSIDER TIP trail in the Coquihalla Canyon Park – it runs on an old rail line through the Othello Tunnels. After a night at the motel in Hope, **take Hwy. 3 up to the Coast Mountains to the wooded ❹ Manning Provincial Park** with its wild rhododendrons blossoming in June (hiking trail to the Rhododendron Flats). **From the 1346 m/4416 ft high Allison Pass, drive down to the sunny east side of the mountain into the valley of the Similkameen River.** Orchards line the route and farmers sell cherries and peaches at roadside stalls. ❺ Osoyoos **near the US border** reminds a bit of a Mediterranean resort with all that bathing in Osoyoos Lake. Interesting: Native American-managed winery Nk'mip Cellars *(1400 Rancher Creek Rd. | tel. 250 4 95 29 85 | Moderate–Expensive)* with cultural centre *(daily 9am – 6pm)*, good restaurant and noble hotel.

The route follows Hwy. 97 north through the 200 km/ 125 mi long ❻ Okanagan Valley → p. 58 – past sandy beaches, orchards and vineyards. Stay at **Penticton** and treat yourself to a trip to the eastern shore of Lake Okanagan

DAY 1–2
❶ Vancouver
45 km/28 mi
❷ Fort Langley
110 km/68 mi
❸ Hope
35 km/21.8 mi
❹ Manning Provincial Park
225 km/140 mi
❺ Osoyoos
32 km/19.9 mi
DAY 3–5
❻ Okanagan Valley

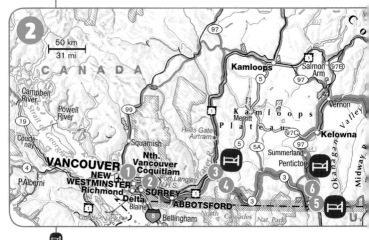

and the numerous wineries of **Naramatha Bench**, all of which have a panoramic view across the lake. From **Vernon** take **Hwys. 6, 31 and 3A** and head further east into the region of the **Arrow Lakes** → p. 61 – barely tapped pioneer country with widely scattered small towns, magnificent provincial parks in a lonely mountainous nature and long and narrow lakes on which car ferries operate. Worthwhile stops along the way: the hot springs of **7 Nakusp** and nearby the small ghost town of **Sandon** from the silver boom period around 1890, **Ainsworth** and **Kokanee Creek Provincial Park**, where you can watch

370 km/230 mi

7 Nakusp

The 135 km/84 mi long Okanagan Lake offers several bathing beaches

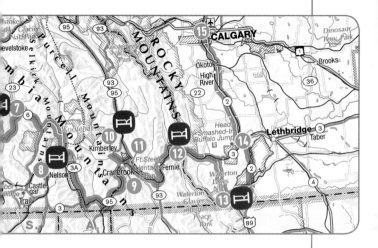

salmon spawn in August. The picturesque old mining town ⑧ **Nelson** is also very nice. A special tip for an overnight stay right in the middle of the town is the stylish, cheerfully renovated **Adventure Hotel** *(39 rooms | 616 Vernon St. | tel. 250 3 52 72 11 | adventurehotel.ca | Moderate)* in an old brick building.

You are again close to the US border. The route continues on Hwys. 3A and 3 (time zone: +1 h) to ⑨ **Cranbrook** (large railway museum) and via ⑩ **Kimberley → p. 78**, the 'Bavarian village' in the Rockies, to the museum town ⑪ **Fort Steele.** On the eastern shore of the Kootenay River you can see the **looming peaks of the Rockies. Hwy. 3 crosses them at an altitude of 1396 m/4450 ft at** ⑫ **Crowsnest Pass → p. 73.** The **Frank Slide Visitor Centre** depicts the hard life of the coal miners in the late 19th century. **At Pincher Creek, the highway heads out into the endless prairie – but first have a detour on Hwy. 6 to the south:** in the lofty mountains of the ⑬ **Waterton Lakes National Park → p. 79.** For the next two days you can enjoy wonderful boat trips and beautiful hiking trails. Head for the **Wieners** *(301 Windflower Ave.)* for great grilled gourmet hotdogs after the hike. On the last day of the route you head out of the mountains and **via the Mormon city Cardston to** ⑭ **Fort Macleod → p. 91** with its excellent Native American Museum **and further north through the ranchland of Alberta** to the end point of the tour, the oil metropolis ⑮ **Calgary → p. 83.**

170 km/106 mi

⑧ Nelson

230 km/143 mi

DAY 6–10

⑨ Cranbrook

27 km/16.8 mi

⑩ Kimberley

37 km/23 mi

⑪ Fort Steele

145 km/90 mi

⑫ Crowsnest Pass

120 km/75 mi

⑬ Waterton Lakes National Park

115 km/71 mi

⑭ Fort Macleod

170 km/106 mi

⑮ Calgary

3 VANCOUVER ISLAND: BEACHES AND RAIN FORESTS

START: ❶ Vancouver
END: ❶ Vancouver

Distance:
🚗 900 km/559 mi

7 days
Driving time
(without stops)
20 hours

COSTS: C$90 for petrol and about C$220 for ferries (car and two people), C$30 for bike rental and C$110 per person for bear watching boat tour in the ❻ Pacific Rim National Park
WHAT TO PACK: Rain jacket, sturdy shoes and bathing suit

IMPORTANT TIPS: Book ferries in advance for weekends during summer and holidays: *www.bcferries.com*.
Refuel on time in the Cariboo region. Gas stations exist only every 50–80 km/30.1–49.7 mi.

A one-week journey, featuring some of the most beautiful impressions of Western Canada. What is best, it is quite feasible in winter too. This is so because the south of Vancouver Island has the mildest climate of anywhere in Canada. This is why ancient rain forests thrive and you find colourful blooming gardens in the provincial capital Victoria.

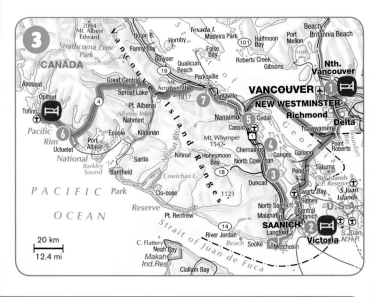

Start in ❶ **Vancouver** → p. 32: You should plan at least one day for the most beautiful metropolis in West Canada: it's time to do some sightseeing in Gastown, on Granville Island and in Robson Street and take a bike tour in Stanley Park – and, naturally, go out for a fine dinner with fresh wild salmon. In South Vancouver, the large **car ferries that are operated by BC Ferries run almost every hour from the ferry terminal in Tsawwassen to** Vancouver Island → p. 40. Keep your eyes open on this trip, for orcas are sometimes seen on this mini cruise through the archipelago of the Gulf Islands. **At the port of Swartz Bay, head south on Hwy. 17 to** ❷ **Victoria** → p. 47, that gorgeous seaside provincial capital of British Columbia, or BC as it is locally called. The casual and fun atmosphere of this town will become evident on your first stroll in the afternoon around the Inner Harbour and the beautiful old town – the motto seems to be 'easy living'. Not to be missed: the totem poles of the Royal BC Museum. The next morning, take a boat trip and do some whale watching, as the islands just off the coast are home to several pods of orcas throughout the summer. How about a bike ride through the lush residential area of Victoria in the afternoon? Bike rental is available at the shop Sports Rent *(1950 Government St.)*. If you like hiking, then take a trip to INSIDER TIP **East Sooke Park, which is just an hour's drive west of downtown (you get there via Hwy. 14 and East Sooke Road). This is where a beautiful trail starts from the Pike Road parking lot and leads to wonderfully secluded bays.**

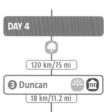
Mural in Chemainus

Continue your trip on the Trans-Canada Highway. Just on the outskirts of Victoria is the Goldstream Park. In fall, salmon swim there to their spawning grounds – and then die in the shallows – it is an impressive spectacle of nature. **Continue north: pass the 350 m/1148 ft Malahat Summit that offers panoramic views across the sea and then head for** ❸ **Duncan** → p. 42 that hosts a myriad of totem poles. **Continue**

DAY 1
❶ Vancouver

DAY 2–3

115 km/71 mi

❷ Victoria

DAY 4

120 km/75 mi

❸ Duncan

18 km/11.2 mi

| ④ Chemainus | 🏛 |
| 35 km/21.8 mi |

| ⑤ Nanaimo | 🍴 |
| 80 km/49.7 mi |

| ⑥ Pacific Rim National Park | 🌲 🚶 🚐 |

| **DAY 5–6** |

| **DAY 7** |
| 400 km/249 mi |

| ⑦ Rathtrevor Provincial Park | 🏖 🚶 |
| 155 km/96 mi |

| ① Vancouver | 🚢 |

on the route to ④ Chemainus, famous for its murals that were created by internationally renowned artists. Make another stop at ⑤ **Nanaimo → p. 43** for a nice stroll on the harbour and some fish and chips at Trollers *(104 Front St. | Budget)*, a popular hangout at the harbour bridge. **Follow Hwys. 19 and 4 for just under three hours to the west coast of Vancouver Island:** to the ⑥ **Pacific Rim National Park → p. 44**. Tip for relaxing on the way: Cathedral Grove, a grove of huge, ancient Douglas fir trees. It is recommended you find an accommodation in the former fishing village **Tofino** on the edge of a national park. The accommodation with the most beautiful view certainly is the cosy INSIDER TIP **Middle Beach Lodge** *(64 rooms | 400 MacKenzie Beach Rd. | tel. 250 7 25 29 00 | www.middlebeach.com | Moderate)*. Use the two days for a walk along **Long Beach**, a boat tour for bear watching, a hike on the **Wild Pacific Trail** in **Ucluelet** – and maybe for a half-day surf course. **Take Hwys. 4 and 19 back to the east coast of the island.** Go for another dip on the sandy beaches of Qualicum Beach or take a walk on the beach in ⑦ **Rathtrevor Provincial Park**. In the afternoon, **take the ferry from Nanaimo** back to ① **Vancouver**.

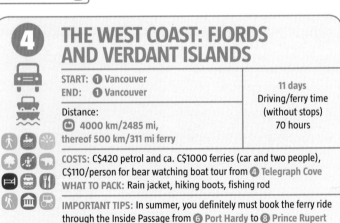

④ THE WEST COAST: FJORDS AND VERDANT ISLANDS

START: ① Vancouver
END: ① Vancouver

11 days
Driving/ferry time
(without stops)
70 hours

Distance:
🚗 4000 km/2485 mi,
thereof 500 km/311 mi ferry

COSTS: C$420 petrol and ca. C$1000 ferries (car and two people), C$110/person for bear watching boat tour from ④ Telegraph Cove
WHAT TO PACK: Rain jacket, hiking boots, fishing rod

IMPORTANT TIPS: In summer, you definitely must book the ferry ride through the Inside Passage from ⑥ Port Hardy to ⑧ Prince Rupert in advance: *www.bcferries.com*.

The destinations of this route are the rugged Pacific coast along the famous Inside Passage and the little explored northern part of British Columbia. A tour into the realm of Native Americans, loggers and pioneer farmers.

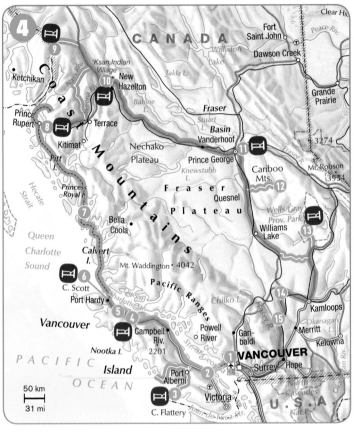

The car ferries leave from the ferry terminal Horseshoe Bay on the northern edge of ① Vancouver → p. 32 to Vancouver Island → p. 40 At the port of destination ② Nanaimo → p. 43 that has a very pretty harbour promenade, **take Hwys. 19 and 4 and head for the beautiful** ③ Pacific Rim National Park → p. 44. The small town of **Tofino** at the end of Hwy. 4 here is the best location to stay for two nights: for beach walks, and maybe a boat ride or kayak trip.

On the east coast, the route follows Hwy. 19 via Campbell River → p. 41 to the north of Vancouver Island. Do not miss: a whale watching tour from ④ Telegraph

DAY 1–4

① Vancouver
80 km/49.7 mi
② Nanaimo
170 km/106 mi
③ Pacific Rim National Park
680 km/423 mi
④ Telegraph Cove
40 km/24.9 mi

Where salmon jump and bears wait with great appetite: Fish Creek

⑤ Alert Bay 🏛
55 km/34.2 mi

DAY 5–6
⑥ Port Hardy ⛴

⑦ Inside Passage 🚌🚶❄
520 km/323 mi

⑧ Prince Rupert 🚡🚶🏛⛴

Cove → p. 47 and a **ferry trip to ⑤ Alert Bay** → p. 46 with its Native American reservation museum and its magnificent collection of totem poles and Native American masks. After a night in **⑥ Port Hardy** → p. 46: **embark for the ride through the ⑦ Inside Passage** → p. 46 – with a little luck with sunshine. It often rains along the sparsely populated coastline as the steep Coast Mountains capture the pacific clouds. That is exactly why towering Douglas fir and Sitka spruce thrive in the island labyrinth and on the mainland of the fjords, creating a unique forest. You can often watch whales, seals and bald eagles from the ferry. **You will reach ⑧ Prince Rupert** → p. 65 **after 15 hours**. The ferry port is in the land of the Tsimshian tribe. Large totem poles throughout the city testify to their carving skills. Stay a day in Prince Rupert: for a morning tour of bear watching in the **Khutzemateen reserve** with Prince Rupert Adventure Tours → p. 65, in the afternoon for the **North Pacific Cannery** *(July/Aug daily 10am–5pm, spring and autumn closed on Mon | admission C$16)* in the suburb of **Port Edward**, which impressively documents the long tradition of fishing in the region.

DAY 7–9
490 km/304 mi

Continue on Hwy. 16, the Yellowhead Highway → p. 64. It runs along the often clouded Skeena River. **Plan a trip to Alaska from Terrace: it's a half-day trip on the Nisga'a**

and **Cassiar Highway** leads to the town of ⑨ **Stewart →
p. 65**, that is located right on the border to the neighbouring country. The mini-village **Hyder** has rustic pubs
and is visited in summer by the bears that come to **Fish
Creek**, located on the outskirts of this village, to catch
salmon. Accommodation tip in Stewart: the historic **Ripley Creek Inn → p. 65**. **Head back to Cassiar Highway
and then south to** ⑩ **Hazelton**, which is an important
settlement centre of the Tsimshian Native Americans. It
is them who operate the highly interesting **K'san Outdoor Museum**. Stop for the night shortly after this museum in **Smithers**. Lonely forests and lakes, only now and
then a small village – the **ride on the Yellowhead Highway** is really long and seems to stretch out forever. The
next day, dead conifers on the roadside are witness to
the frantic spread of the bark beetle. South of the lumberjack town ⑪ **Prince George → p. 64**, the seemingly
endless forests have suffered even more – huge forest
fires raged here as recently as 2017. (You can connect to
Route 1 on Hwy. 16 and continue to the Rockies.)

Head south on Hwy. 97, the Cariboo Highway, through
the sunny ranch land of the Cariboo Region → p. 51. Not
to be missed: the old gold mining town ⑫ **Barkerville
→ p. 51**, which today is completely preserved as a Ghost
Town Museum and a site of historic interest. **From the
100 Mile House, take Hwys. 24 and 5 to Clearwater and
the** ⑬ **Wells Gray Provincial Park → p. 62**, which is famous for its waterfalls and lakes. Take the time for a canoe trip on Clearwater Lake → p. 118. On the way back,
**take Hwy. 5 back to civilisation and to the mostly sunny
and hot ranchland around Kamloops → p. 56**. In the valley of the Thompson River, **the Trans-Canada Highway
meanders** westwards. The interior of BC is almost desert-like dry and looks like a country taken from a Western
movie. Visit ⑭ **INSIDERTIP Hat Creek Ranch** (May–Sept
daily 9am–5pm | admission C$13.50) near Cache Creek:
a authentic and very photogenic coaching inn. Continue
from ⑮ **Lytton → p. 57** (where you still have time for a
rafting trip) **on the Trans-Canada Highway, which follows the Fraser River to the sea.** The mighty river has
carved a deep canyon through the Coast Mountains. The
narrowest and wildest section of the river is from south
of Lytton up to shortly before Hope. Dense forests cover
the hillsides and accompany **Hwy. 1 through the widening Fraser Valley back to** ① **Vancouver**.

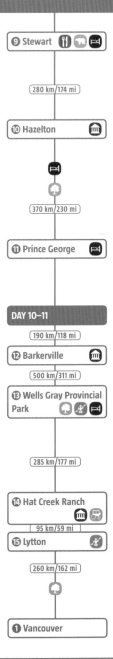

⑨ Stewart

280 km / 174 mi

⑩ Hazelton

370 km / 230 mi

⑪ Prince George

DAY 10–11

190 km / 118 mi

⑫ Barkerville

500 km / 311 mi

⑬ Wells Gray Provincial Park

285 km / 177 mi

⑭ Hat Creek Ranch

95 km / 59 mi

⑮ Lytton

260 km / 162 mi

① Vancouver

⑤ YUKON: THE GOLDEN ROUTE

START: ① Skagway, Alaska END: ⑦ Dawson City, Yukon	21 days
Distance: 53 km/32.9 mi hiking, 120 km/75 mi bus/train, 736 km/457 mi canoe	

COSTS: Hiking permit about C$50 per person; train/bus C$100, 1 week canoe rental C$400 plus C$80 one-way fee

WHAT TO PACK: Supplies, camping and full hiking equipment

IMPORTANT TIPS: Best travel time: July/Aug. The trail requires a permit from the *park service*. Registration and information at *www.nps.gov/klgo*. Reservation recommended. In summer, a railbus service runs for hikers from ④ Bennett to ⑤ Whitehorse: *wpyr.com*.

Pure adventure. Follow the original route of the early prospectors to the Klondike on foot and by canoe and tent: across the legendary Chilkoot Pass and down the Yukon to Dawson City. It sounds like a lot, but the 736 km/457 mi canoe tour is INSIDERTIP suitable even for beginners because you comfortably drift along with the river. The 53 km/32.9 mi long hike at the beginning is much more strenuous. Alternatively, you can do it – as the entire tour – by car.

DAY 1–5
① Skagway

The journey starts, as it once did for the pioneers, in Alaska in ① Skagway. **You can easily reach it by ferry or plane from the south and by bus from Whitehorse.** As in the old days, the little town is the last feeding station on the way into the hinterland. In the winter of 1898, 30,000 adventurers journeyed from Skagway across the mountains to

The historic Chilkoot Trail leads from sea level to above the tree line

the north and in the following spring to the Yukon River and on to the Klondike gold fields. **The route of the historic ❷ Chilkoot Trail as well as the parallel running modern highway largely runs through pristine wilderness to this day.** Today, a **hike across the 1067 m/3501 ft high ❸ Chilkoot Pass** takes four to five days, but now you can reserve a tent – what a difference to the efforts of the pioneers: prospectors had to haul a ton of luggage across the pass, enough food and equipment for a full year. Mounties of the Canadian police checked at the summit of the pass whether each pioneer had brought the demanded quantity. The pioneers had to climb the steep ridge of the Coast Mountains 30 or 40 times to laboriously haul the luggage up. In the dead of winter! This may be an incentive for todays hikers who work up a gentle summer sweat under a super-light high-tech backpack when crossing the pass... but only once, that is. The end point of the Chilkoot Trail is ❹ Bennett. **Continue by train and bus via Carcross to ❺ Whitehorse → p. 99.**

Take a day of rest in the town of Whitehorse. In the paddle steamer **S.S. Klondike → p. 99** in **Miles Canyon** you can learn more about the historical sites of the gold rush era and stock up your supplies. Then head further north. Now it becomes very authentic as you travel by canoe, because even the prospectors of the past used rafts and self-made boats and confided themselves to the Yukon River to drift downstream northward to the promised land of gold. Today, this route can be made by canoe in about 15 days even without great wilderness experience. Canoe rentals and suppliers can be found in Whitehorse and guided tours are organised by **Ruby Range** (www.rubyrange.com). **Slowly drifting down the wide Yukon, paddling through the ❻ Lake Labarge**, observing moose and bear, trying (mostly unsuccessful) to catch some fish, most often **Five Finger Rapids**, making campfires on the shore and enjoying the tranquillity of nature. Until you finally join civilisation again **where the Klondike River meets the Yukon**: the town of ❼ **Dawson City → p. 95** – the desired destination at the end of the Golden Trail.

❷ Chilkoot Trail

[38 km/23.6 mi]

❸ Chilkoot Pass

[24 km/14.9 mi]

❹ Bennett

[120 km/75 mi]

❺ Whitehorse

DAY 6–21

[50 km/31.1 mi]

❻ Lake Labarge

[686 km/426 mi]

❼ Dawson City

SPORTS & ACTIVITIES

Thanks to the pioneers, the outdoor life-style is a way of life for Canadians. So it is not surprising that even today every sport is enthusiastically enjoyed out in the fresh air. This is particularly true on the west coast, where smoking is frowned upon and fitness is the new religion. It is also made easy for visitors as every major hotel and holiday resort has their own fitness centre and an activity desk, where you can book tee-off times for the on-site golf course and obtain information about other activities. Several rental shops in parks and cities rent out canoes, bicycles and other sporting equipment – along with tips and maps. Organised day tours can also be booked at short notice. However, excursions that are several days long are best booked in advance.

The canoe was invented in Canada. You can rent canoes in many lodges. Sea kayaking tours in the west coast island labyrinth and rubber dinghy trips are popular.

CLEARWATER LAKE TOURS

Good canoe rentals and trips on the large, secluded lakes of the Wells Gray Provincial Park. *Clearwater | tel. 250 6 74 21 21 | www.clearwaterlaketours.com*

SUNWOLF

Full-day rubber dinghy boat trips on the Elaho River near Whistler. For families, there are halfday and much more gentle float trips available. *70002 Squamish*

Horseback riding, hiking, canoeing: the rugged Pacific coastline and the peaks of the Rockies offer an ideal destination for outdoor sports

Valley Rd. | Brackendale | tel. 604 8 98 15 37 | www.sunwolf.net

INSIDER TIP ▶ TIMBERWOLF TOURS
Multi-day guided canoe trips and adventure tours in the Rockies. *Site 34, 51404 RR264 | Spruce Grove | Alberta | tel. 780 4 70 49 66 | timberwolftours.com*

CYCLING

Bicycles for day trips *(around C$20–40 per day, C$70–150 per week)* are readily available in the towns of the south. For longer rides, the Gulf Islands off Vancouver and the Okanagan Valley are ideal as are the old railway tracks in the Kettle Valley and the Rockies – here, however, you do need to be quite fit. For mountain bike enthusiasts there is the annual *Trans-Rockies Bike Race (www. transrockies.com)*.

SOUL SKI & BIKE

In summer, bike rentals and one-and several-day tours in Banff National Park and on Icefields Parkway. *203 A Bear St. Banff | tel. 403 760 16 50 | banffsoul.com*

WHISTLER MOUNTAIN BIKE PARK

The ultimate playground for mountain bikers: summer lifts and a 1200 m/3937 ft difference in altitude; mid-July *Bike Festival. Whistler | tel. 800 766 04 49 | bike. whistlerblackcomb.com*

FISHING

Most anglers dream about Pacific salmon but the fun is not cheap: from C$500 for two days and up to C$10,000 for a week in an exclusive fishing resort. Amateur anglers may fish anywhere as long as they have a licence *(C$20–100 depending on permit period)* and they are available in sporting goods stores and lodges.

APRIL POINT LODGE

A dream location for salmon fishermen actually exists in this lodge surrounded by rocks, waves and woods near Campbell River well-stocked with fish in the archipelago near Vancouver Island *Quadra Island | tel. 250 2 85 22 22 | www. aprilpoint.com*

GOLF

Golf is popular in Canada and there are many golf courses. The greens are mostly open to the public. Also non-club members without a handicap are welcome and green fees are affordable (C$50–100).

The most beautiful and expensive courses are in the Rockies, such as the legendary Fairmont Course in Banff or Jasper National Park and those in Invermere or Kananaskis. The sites *www. albertagolf.org, www.golftherockies.net* and *www.britishcolumbiagolf.org* have more info.

HIKING

The largest selection of trails – signposted and well maintained – are in the national and provincial parks. Wardens in the visitor centres are helpful and provide information about the best trails. Good path networks exist e.g. in Banff, Yoho and Jasper national parks. Hiking outside of the parks is often difficult – in Canada, wilderness really does mean wilderness.

RIDING

Anyone can do it. You don't need to be experienced as they use Western style saddles and the horses walk very obediently in a row. Rides can be booked at many ranches at short notice. Experienced riders can book ranch holidays and ride with the cowboys all day long. Info: *www.bcguestranches.com* and *www. albertacountryvacation.com*

RANGEVIEW RANCH

Rustic *working ranch* in the Rockies near Waterton Lakes Park. *Box 28, Site 10 | Cardston | tel. 403 6 53 28 21 | www. rangeviewranch.com*

INSIDER TIP TEN-EE-AH LODGE

Well maintained log cabin lodge with horseback riding program and other activities in British Columbia. There is also a campsite. *Lac La Hache | tel. 250 4 34 97 45 | www.ten-ee-ah.bc.ca*

ROPE COURSES & ZIP LINES

Adrenaline rush: in recent years rope and adventure courses for adults (and children) have been popping up throughout Canada. Zip lining through canyons and over streams or above the forest has become a popular activity. All

All major national parks have magnificent hiking trails of all difficulty levels

the guides are trained and the equipment is safe and well secured – guaranteed fun. For an overview: *www.zipline rider.com* and *www.wildplay.com*

WELLNESS

Yoga, massages, whirlpool baths – every better holiday hotel in Western Canada has long since recognised the trend and offers a spa and always a fitness centre too. The Fairmont Hotels even have their own spa luxury brand with the *Willow Stream Spa*. There are also day spas (independent from hotels) in the cities where you can book a single yoga lesson or a massage. For a good selection check out the website *www. leadingspasofcanada.com*.

WINTER SPORTS

The powder snow in the Rocky Mountains is legendary. Ski areas such as Banff, Lake Louise, Fernie, or Big White offer excellent ski slopes. The largest winter sports area is Whistler on the west coast.

Experienced skiers can also enjoy the – admittedly not very environmentally friendly – thrill of heli-skiing in central British Columbia.

CANADIAN MOUNTAIN HOLIDAYS

Organised heli-skiing trips into the remote mountains on the western edge of the Rocky Mountains. *Banff | tel. 403 762 7100 | www.canadianmountain holidays.com*

TRAVEL WITH KIDS

Canada is also a very child-friendly country. The Canadians themselves travel with their offspring during the holiday months of July and August and the tourist infrastructure is geared for families. In the restaurants there are special children's menus and child seats. Most hotels offer children's beds and cots – sometimes at no additional cost – and many motels have paddling pools for the little ones next to the main swimming pool.

All activities on the sea and the lakes are fun. Canoeing, for instance, is a lot of fun and there are lakes around every corner. Ghost towns and trapper forts are there to be explored and many places have their own children's museum. Travelling in a mobile home is also very popular: the vehicle creates a familiar, consistent environment while the outdoors and camping offer real adventure, making your holiday in Canada a success.

VANCOUVER

INSIDER TIP ▶ GRANVILLE ISLAND KIDS MARKET (U B5–6) (*m b5–6*)

A whole warehouse full of toys, fun crayons, colourful sweets and other temptations. Just across the road is a large model train museum. *Daily 10am–6pm | Granville Island | www.kidsmarket.ca*

MINIATURE TRAIN, WATER PARK AND SECOND BEACH POOL

(U C1, A2) (*m c1, a2*)

The large city parks provide a variety of activities for children in summer: the

Holidays in Canada are great for children – spotting bears and eagles by day, toasting marshmallows around the campfire by night

water park at *Lumberman's Arch (daily 10am–6pm | admission free)* offers spray fountains, water cannons and a narrow gauge railway, and at *Second Beach (families C$3/per person)* there is a large heated outdoor pool with water slide and children's area. *Stanley Park*

SCIENCE WORLD (U E–F5) *(ﾏﾏ e-f5)*
The Expo 86 sphere is now a children's technology museum with interactive experiments and a surround screen cinema. *Mon–Fri 10am–5pm, Sat/Sun 10am–6pm | admission C$26.75, children C$22 | 1455 Quebec St. | www.scienceworld.ca*

VANCOUVER ISLAND

INSIDER **HORNE LAKE CAVES PROV. PARK** (144 C5) *(ﾏﾏ E14)*
Mine lamps light the way into the park's mysterious caves and there is quite a lot to see for young and old including fossils, crystal formations, waterfalls and stalactites and stalagmites. *Guided tour C$27, children 5 years and older permitted,*

also longer tours | reservation: tel. 250 2 48 78 29 | www.hornelake.com | 25 km/15.5 mi north-west of Parksville

MCLEAN MILL (144 C5) (*$\varnothing$ E14*)

Take a steam train through the forest to an old steam-powered sawmill. You will be briefed like a new worker 100 years ago. *Wed–Sun 10am–4pm, Thu–Sun journey by steam train and steam operation of the sawmill | admission C$10, children C$5, steam train C$35, children C$25 | E & N train station | 3100 Kingsway | Port Alberni | mcleanmill.ca*

MINIATURE WORLD (144 C6) (*$\varnothing$ E15*)

The Empress Hotel has a museum full of dollhouses and miniature scenes from fairytales and children's books. *Daily in summer 9am–9pm, otherwise 9am–5pm | admission C$12, children C$8 | 649 Humboldt St. | Victoria*

Dressed and ready for the powwow

QUINSAM RIVER HATCHERY (144 B4) (*$\varnothing$ E13*)

Millions of young salmon are held in large ponds and rearing channels before being released to spawn in late summer and autumn. *5 km/3.1 mi northwest of Campbell River. Daily 8.15am–4pm | admission free | 4217 Argonaut Rd.*

BRITISH COLUMBIA

KOOTENAY RIVER RUNNERS (146 B4) (*$\varnothing$ J13*)

Adventurous rafting on the Kicking Horse and the Kootenay rivers and the shorter Toby Creek (children over 8 years of age). *From C$62, children from C$52 | Hwy. 93 | Radium Hot Springs | tel. 250 3 47 92 10 | www.raftingtherockies.com*

PENTICTON CHANNEL (145 E5) (*$\varnothing$ G14*)

Floating down the channel between the two lakes in Penticton on an inner tube is a lot of fun. *Coyote Cruises (tel. 250 4 92 2115) rent out tubes (approx. C$12) and organise transport back. Hwy. 97 at the northern end of the channel*

ZIPTREK ECOTOURS $\bigcirc$ (145 D4) (*$\varnothing$ F13*)

One of the oldest and most experienced zip line companies in the world, children from 6 years are taken along in tandem rides. The platforms and zip lines are designed in such a way that they do not have an impact on the forest nature. *Whistler | tel. 866 9 35 00 01 | www.ziptrek.com*

ROCKY MOUNTAINS

LUXTON MUSEUM (146 B4) (*$\varnothing$ J13*)

The Native American museum is interesting for smaller children, showing feather jewellery craft and how to construct a teepee. *Daily in summer 10am–7pm, otherwise 11am–5pm | admission C$10, children C$5 | 1 Birch Ave. | Banff*

ALBERTA

ALBERTA BIRDS OF PREY CENTRE
(146 C5) (*∭ L14*)
A sanctuary for birds of prey where injured hawks, owls and eagles are nursed back to health. Flying demonstration every 90 minutes. *Daily in summer 9.30am–5pm | admission C$12, children C$8 | Coaldale/ Lethbridge | www.burrowingowl.com*

CALGARY ZOO & PREHISTORIC PARK
(146 C4) (*∭ K13*)
A zoo with Siberian tigers and the indigenous animals of Canada. The main attraction is the 'Jurassic Park' with 20 lifesized dinosaurs. *Daily 9am–5pm | admission C$25, children C$17 | 1300 Zoo Rd. NE | Calgary | www.calgaryzoo.org*

RAFTER SIX RANCH (146 B4) (*∭ K13*)
Good for a family day out: riding on horses and ponies, horse-drawn carriage rides and rafting tours in a beautiful setting. *Seebe | tel. 403 6 73 36 22 | www. raftersix.com*

ROYAL TYRRELL MUSEUM OF
PALEONTOLOGY ★ (146 C4) (*∭ L13*)
The palaeontology museum offers excavations for different age groups under the guidance of scientists. There are also INSIDER TIP special guided tours for children. *Daily in summer 9am–9pm | admission C$18, children C$10, programmes from C$10 | 1500 N Dinosaur Trail | Drumheller | tel. 403 8 23 77 07 | www.tyrrell museum.com*

WEST EDMONTON MALL/GALAXYL-
AND AMUSEMENT PARK
(146 C2) (*∭ K11*)
The world's largest indoor amusement park with roller coaster rides, carousels and a 3D cinema. It also features numerous other attractions for children: large wave pool with slides, ice skating rink, climbing course, mini golf and shows with sea lions. *Daily in summer from 10am | day ticket for children C$35, also single rides | 87th Ave./170th St. | Edmonton | www.wem.ca*

Large head, sharp teeth: a fierce Albertosaurus in the Royal Tyrrell Museum

NORTHERN CANADA

YUKON WILDLIFE PRESERVE
(138 C5) (*∭ C4*)
An ideal opportunity to see the animals of the north: elk, bison, caribou and a dozen other animal species live here in large enclosures. *Daily in summer 9.30am–6pm | admission C$20, children C$11 | Takhini Hot Springs Rd. | Whitehorse | www.yukonwildlife.ca*

FESTIVALS & EVENTS

In summer every cultural group and village celebrates its own events alongside major festivals: pioneer days, lumberjack competitions, rodeos and Native American powwows, but also folk and music festivals. Visit the local visitor's centre for what is being celebrated where.

FESTIVALS

FEBRUARY

Whitehorse: **Sourdough Rendezvous** with **Frostbite Music Festival:** winterly gold diggers' festival for the famous 1500 km/932 mi long dog sled race the **Yukon Quest**; www.yukonquest.com

MAY

Vancouver: rodeo in Cloverdale; www.cloverdalerodeo.com
Victoria: on **Victoria Day** parades, concerts, races. Following weekend: **Swiftsure Race**

JUNE

Vancouver: the Chinese **Dragon Boat Festival** in mid June; then the famous **Vancouver International Jazz Festival**
High River, **Guy Weadick Days:** pioneer wagon races in mid June

JULY

Canada Day: 1 July, Canada's national day – picnics, parades. Williams Lake – **Rodeo**, Dawson City – gold panning competition and **River Quest Canoe Race**; www.yukonriverquest.com
Calgary: early July – world's largest rodeo, the ★ **Calgary Stampede**; www.calgarystampede.com
Nanaimo, **Marine Festival and Bathtub Race:** end of July – bathtub boats paddle to Vancouver; www.bathtubbing.com
Yellowknife, **Folk on the Rocks:** 24 hours of music under the midnight sun, mid July; folkontherocks.com
Vancouver, **Celebration of Light:** fireworks competition in the harbour
Medicine Hat, INSIDER TIP **Exhibition & Stampede:** car racing, rodeo, etc. (last weekend of July); www.mhstampede.com

JULY–AUGUST

July – late August: artists meet for **Banff Arts Festival** concerts, theatre, and ballet

AUGUST

Squamish, ★ **Squamish Days Loggers Sports:** lumberjacks display their skill

Rodeos and axe contests: in summer the long weekends are especially popular for festivals and events

and stamina on the first weekend in August; *squamishdays.ca*

Vancouver Island: lumberjacks compete with their axes at the Campbell River ● *Salmon Festival*

Lethbridge, ***Whoop-Up Days:*** middle of the month there is the famous folk festival and rodeo

Abbotsford, ***International Air Show:*** historical aircraft (middle of the month); *www.abbotsfordairshow.com*

Dawson City, ★ ***Discovery Days:*** on the 17th Aug. the town celebrates the discovery of gold in the Yukon

Vancouver, ***Pacific National Exhibition:*** agricultural show and fair with concerts and rides; *www.PNE.ca*

SEPTEMBER

Dawson City: on the first weekend participants in the INSIDERTIP ***Klondike International Outhouse Race*** drive through the town with decorated toilets on wheels

Kelowna: the wineries of the Okanagan Valley host the ***Fall Wine Festival***; *www.thewinefestivals.com*

PUBLIC HOLIDAYS

1st Jan	New Year's Day
March/April	Good Friday, Easter
Mon before 25 May	
	Victoria Day
1st July	Canada Day
1st Mon in Aug	
	National Holiday (in British Columbia and Alberta)
3rd Mon in Aug	
	Discovery Day (in Yukon Territory)
1st Mon in Sept	
	Labour Day
2nd Mon in Oct	
	Thanksgiving
11 Nov	Remembrance Day
25/26 Dec	Christmas

LINKS, BLOGS, APPS & MORE

www.Canada.travel A comprehensive site that includes places to go, things to do, trip ideas and videos. Also recommendations by specially trained travel agents with experience in Canada

www.parkscanada.ca Great website with detailed descriptions of the individual national parks. The site includes videos, 3D representations and features such as an interactive map where you select your region for specials and highlights

www.weather.gc.ca Official Canadian weather service with satellite imagery, rain radar – and surprisingly accurate weather forecasts for even the smallest town in this massive country

www.aboriginalbc.com Site promoting cultural tourism with Native American offerings including lodges, canoe trips and cultural centres

maps.Google.com Everybody knows Google Maps. Street view for Whistler and the Rockies also shows ski slopes!

www.travel.bc.ca An excellent resource for accommodation, activities and tours and there are also great discount deals and featured listings

www.straight.com/blogra The comprehensive online blog of Vancouver's Georgia Straight newspaper – features and articles on nightlife, art etc.

ibackpackcanada.com Independent travel guide written by Corbin Fraser. Ideal travel blog for those travelling through Canada on a budget

www.Whistler.com/blog News on the sports scene in Whistler. Events, etc.

cbcmusic.ca/#/radio3/blogs All about the Canadian music scene, indie bands and mainstream, upcoming concerts etc.

Regardless of whether you are still reaserching your trip or already in Western Canada: these addresses will provide you with more information, videos and networks to make your holiday even more enjoyable

www.airbnb.com An online booking site for guesthouses and private accommodation with lots of listings for Western Canada.

www.9flats.com A little more expensive, this site lists private accommodation (search under the town where you would like to stay over). There are listings for houses, apartments and rooms (even an igloo)

@mec_vancouver Meetup announcements and contacts for group races, SUP or kayak training from the largest sports shop in Vancouver

www.cbc.ca/north Winter in the Arctic? Or summer? Short films, photos and news articles portray life in the Yukon and the Northwest Territories

www.yukonquest.com Everything you need to know about the world's hardest and longest sled dog race; with videos and live tracking

www.much.com Music videos and interviews with Canadian pop and rock stars from the most important music station in the country

www.5min.com Extensive video selection with numerous short films about Canada – search under travel and select the respective province or city name

Visit Vancouver A tour through the city, interactive dining options, upcoming and current events, photos and videos for iPad

Live Nation Information and ticket centre for concert tours, clubs and venues in Vancouver or Calgary. Details at www.livenation.com

OpenTable A useful application for restaurant reservations, with a good selection (especially in the cities) of restaurants; you can also use it to find restaurants closest to your current location and see what tables are available, last minute reservations are often an option

TRAVEL TIPS

ARRIVAL

✈ Air Canada and most national carriers have regular direct flights to Vancouver or to Calgary with domestic flight connections to all the major cities. Other indirect locations such as Edmonton and Whitehorse can also be reached via connecting flights also with other European airlines including Iceland Air.
In the peak tourist season (July and Aug) flights are often fully booked, so you should book as early as possible – several months in advance – this also applies for the trans-Atlantic route, for motor homes and the longer ferry passages.

CAMPING & YOUTH HOSTELS

Canada's public camping sites are beautiful, they are usually situated next to the water in national parks and they all have a fireplace, wooden benches, water pump and a simple outhouse and cost

RESPONSIBLE TRAVEL

It doesn't take a lot to be environmentally friendly whilst travelling. Don't just think about your carbon footprint whilst flying to and from your holiday destination, but also about how you can protect nature and culture abroad. As a tourist it is especially important to respect nature, look out for local products, cycle instead of driving, save water and much more. If you would like to find out more about eco-tourism please visit: www.ecotourism.org

C$10–40 per night. Private, luxuriously equipped sites can be found on the outskirts of cities and outside the national parks (prices approx. C$20–50). Camping rough is not prohibited (except in the parks), but is frowned upon in the populated areas. Camping spaces in national parks can be booked beforehand at www.reservation.pc.gc.ca, other parks in BC, www.discovercamping.ca.
The accommodation by the Canadian Hostelling Association (www.hihostels.ca) costs from C$15 per night, some also have single and double rooms available from C$40. In the large cities backpackers can stay at the YMCA (for men) and the YWCA (for women), in the countryside you will often find small home hostels.

CAR HIRE

The major car rental companies like Alamo, Avis and Hertz have representatives at all airports. An even better option is for you to first go into the city and then collect the vehicle the next morning – well-rested for your first trip with the unfamiliar vehicle. The minimum age to rent a car is 21, often 25 years. Your national driving licence will suffice. You should book cars or camper vans through a travel agent several months in advance, this is usually cheaper and safer. One-way routes often mean penalties.

CONSULATES & EMBASSIES

U.S CONSULATE GENERAL VANCOUVER
1095 W Pender Street | Vancouver | BC V6E 2M6 | tel. +1 604 6 85 43 11 | ca.usembassy.gov/embassy-consulates/vancouver

From arrival to weather

BRITISH CONSULATE-GENERAL VANCOUVER

Suite 800, 1111 Melville Street | Vancouver | BC V6E 3V6 | tel. +1 604 6 83 44 21 | www.gov.uk/world/organisations/british-consulate-general-vancouver

AUSTRALIAN CONSULATE IN VANCOUVER

Suite 2050-1075 | West Georgia Street | Vancouver | BC V6E 3C9 | tel. +1 604 6 94 61 60 | www.canada.embassy.gov.au

CUSTOMS

The following goods can be imported duty free into Canada: 1.1 litres of spirits, 200 cigarettes, 50 cigars or 250g tobacco, 50g perfume or 250g eau de toilette and gifts up to a value of C$60. Plants and foodstuffs (especially fresh food) may not be imported.

DOMESTIC FLIGHTS

Air Canada and some regional airlines offer fares discounted by 40 % for routes within Canada. But you should better buy these tickets in advance of your trip. Otherwise, flights on regional airlines such as Air North and West Jet are most of the time cheaper when purchased online.

DRIVING

You can drive with your national driving license for up to three months (Yukon: 1 month). In all provinces it is compulsory to wear seatbelts and it is best to refrain from drinking and driving. On the major roads the maximum speed is 80 km/50 mi or 100 km/62 mi, in towns 50 km/31 mi and on motorways 110 km/68 mi.

Traffic regulations are standard but there are certain unusual features: at the traffic light you can also turn right on red, on multi-lane roads you may overtake, but schoolbuses with their

BUDGETING

Coffee	£1.60–2.70/US$2.20–3.70	*for a pot of coffee*
Beer	£3.50–5.40/US$4.90–7.40	*for a beer in a restaurant*
Salmon	£11–22/US$15–30	*for a piece*
Boots	£105–115/US$145–160	*for original cowboy boots*
Petrol	£0.80–0.85/US$1.10–1.17	*for a litre unleaded*
Canoe	£13–22/US$18.50–30	*rental for one hour*

hazard lights on may never be passed, not even from the opposite side. The *Canadian Automobile Club (CAA)* also helps members of foreign clubs (identity required; emergency number: *tel. 800 2 22 43 57*).

ELECTRICITY

Current is 110 volts, 60Ht. Mobile phones, tablets and appliances such as shavers and hair dryers from other countries will need a transformer and you will also need a plug adaptor for Canada's two-pin sockets.

EMERGENCY SERVICES

Dial *911* or *0* for the operator

FERRIES

Ferries travel hourly between Vancouver Island and the mainland and do not require advance booking. Expect waiting times on weekends and during summer. However, you will need to book early for the 15 hour trip between Port Hardy and Prince Rupert through the Inside Passage (in a travel agency).

For further information once you are in Canada: *tel. 250 3 86 34 31 or 1 88 82 23 37 79 | www.bcferries.com*

HEALTH

Medical care in Canada is very good – but expensive. A day in hospital can cost C$1000 or more. Ensure you have foreign health insurance. You can buy medicine in a pharmacy or drugstore. A concern in summer are mosquitos. Stock up insect repellents and sprays and wear trousers and long sleeved shirts when hiking.

IMMIGRATION

Tourists from the US, EU and most Commonwealth countries (UK, Australia and New Zealand) require a valid machine-readable passport. Since 2016, also an *Electronic Travel Authorization (ETA)*, which is valid for five years and available for C$9 at *www.canada.ca/eta*. Passport holders from other countries must apply for visas. Passports issued after Oct 2006 must contain a data chip. Small children need their own passport even if registered in their parent's passport. The immigration officer at your point of arrival decides your length of stay – generally not longer than six months. To extend your stay after arrival, you must apply for such at the nearest Canada Immigration Centre. Do this well in advance of the expiry of your current authorised date. Check to see if you qualify under the *Visa Waiver Program (VWP)* if you

FOR BOOKWORMS & FILM BUFFS

The Swarm. A Novel of the Deep: – For his 900 pages deep sea thriller, Frank Schätzing researched a lot on the Canadian Pacific Coast and integrated the region in his novel (2006)

Atanarjuat: The Fast Runner – The film poetically and compellingly tells the story of an Inuit myth. It was the first Canadian film to be written, directed and acted in Inuktitut (2001)

River – A great 400-page tome relating the story of life on a farm in Western Canada. Things are idyllic on the small farm until the young charismatic River appears on the scene, setting in motion a chain of dark events. The author Donna Milner is a master of heightening tension (2008).

Forsaken – The first film to combine the two Canadian superstars Donald and Kiefer Sutherland was released just in the year 2015. The age of gunslingers is revived against the background of the prairie and mountains in Alberta.

plan to cross the border into the US: you can travel to the US for 90 days or less without having to obtain a visa.

INFORMATION

The Canadian Tourist Office website *www.canada.travel* provides extensive information about Canada's attractions and activities. There are also competitions and travel ideas. There are links to the individual provinces such as Alberta and British Columbia and you can also request brochures and maps for each region.

More detailed information and suggestions for tours in individual provinces and territories are available on their web sites.

Alberta: *www.travelalberta.com*
British Columbia: *www.britishcolumbia.travel* and *www.hellobv.com*
Yukon: *www.travelyukon.com*

INTERNET & WI-FI

Canada has an excellent network. Hotels often provide free internet access, only luxury hotels charge a fee. Computers in the lobby are often available free of charge. With your own laptop or smart phone you find Wi-Fi (free or with a password from the staff) in many coffee shops. You are also mostly able to surf free of charge and check your e-mails in Visitor Centres and all public libraries.

MONEY & CREDIT CARDS

Local currency is the Canadian dollar (= 100 cents). Bank notes are available in 5, 10, 20, 50 and 100 dollars and coins in ¢1 (penny), ¢5 (nickel), ¢10 (dime), ¢25 (quarter), C$1 (loonie) and C$2 (toonie). Banks usually open from 10am to 3pm.

CURRENCY CONVERTER

£	C$	C$	£
1	1.75	1	0.55
3	5.25	3	1.65
5	8.75	5	2.75
20	35	20	11
40	70	40	22
75	131.25	75	41.25
200	350	200	110
500	875	500	275

C$	US$	US$	C$
1	0.75	1	1.30
3	2.25	3	3.90
5	3.75	5	6.50
20	15	20	26
40	30	40	52
75	56.25	75	97.50
200	150	200	260
500	375	500	650

For current exchange rates see www.xe.com

You can exchange foreign currencies into dollars at airports and major hotels (but the rate may be bad), banks do not change. Divide your holiday fund into various payment methods: approx. C$100 cash for the arrival, a credit card for the majority of daily expenses (Visa or Mastercard is accepted everywhere at petrol stations, restaurants, etc.), as well as a debit cards which you can use to draw cash from most ATMs at a favourable exchange rate. To be extra safe you can also take a few hundred dollars in traveller's cheques (they are accepted in shops and restaurants and you get your change in cash).

MOSQUITOES

These whining monsters can turn hikes and camping holidays into purgatory, particularly in early summer. Luckily, these insects do not transmit any diseases and even the bite of the black flies is unpleasant but not dangerous. The best protection is to use Canadian repellents with containing deet such as Off, Cutter and Muskol.

OPENING HOURS

Shops are usually open Mon–Sat from 9.30am–6pm, large shopping malls, 10am–9pm and Sun noon–5pm. Supermarkets are often open evenings and weekends, in the large cities some are open around the clock. Many museums are closed on Mondays.

PHONE & MOBILE PHONE

Tri- or Quad-Band European mobiles mostly only function in cities and in the South of the Provinces (sometimes high roaming charges). Ask your mobile phone provider about special rates before travelling. It's cheaper to use phone booths or prepaid cards than using your mobile. Cards are available at petrol stations and grocery stores. For a longer stay it is worth getting a Canadian SIM card and using it with your (unlocked!) mobile.

All telephone numbers in Canada have seven digits and a 3-digit prefix for long distance and within some cities (area code). You must always include the area code (local or long distance). The operator (dial 0) will help with any problems and also sets up collect calls. Toll free numbers for hotels or tour booking begin with the prefix *800*, *866*, *877* or *888* Code for the UK: *+44*. US: *+1*. Australia: *+61*, then choose the area code without

WEATHER IN VANCOUVER

	Jan	Feb	March	April	May	June	July	Aug	Sept	Oct	Nov	Dec
Daytime temperatures in °C/°F	6/43	8/46	11/52	14/57	18/64	21/70	23/73	23/73	19/66	14/57	9/48	7/45
Nighttime temperatures in °C/°F	1/34	1/34	3/37	5/41	8/46	11/52	13/55	12/54	10/50	7/45	4/39	2/36
Sunshine hours/day	2	3	4	6	7	7	9	8	6	4	2	1
Precipitation days/month	17	13	14	11	7	5	4	7	7	15	16	18
Water temperature in °C/°F	8	7	8	9	11	13	14	14	13	12	11	10

the first zero and then the number. Code for Canada: *+1*.

POST

Post offices open Mon–Fri 9am–5.30pm and Sat 8am–noon. Postage: airmail letter or postcard to the US is C$1.05 and C$2.50 for international mail (up to 30g).

PUBLIC TRANSPORT

Greyhound and several regional bus lines (e.g. Brewster, Red Arrow Express, Pacific Coach Lines) connect all the larger towns. Information in travel agencies or at *www.greyhound.ca*.

Another wonderful way to see Canada is to travel from coast to coast on the legendary Trans-Canada route from Montréal via Jasper to Vancouver, and there is also the *Rocky Mountaineer* from Calgary via Banff to Vancouver or vice versa (book several months in advance, *www.rockymountaineer.com*). The rail company VIA Rail *(www.viarail.ca)* offers a *Canrailpass* for their entire network.

TAX

Canada has a 5% *Goods and Services Tax (GST)* levied by the federal government and each province has its own *Provincial Sales Tax (PST)*. British Columbia has a PST of 7%. Some taxes are only added to the purchase price at the cash register.

TIME

Canada has multiple time zones. In British Columbia and in the Yukon it is *Pacific Time (PDT)* which is eight hours behind *Coordinated Universal (UTC)*, in the Northwest Territories and Alberta it is *Mountain Time (MDT)* which is six hours behind *Coordinated Universal*

(UTC). Summer time is – different from Europe – from second Sunday in March till first Sunday in November.

TIPPING

A service charge is not included in the restaurants and the standard tip is 15–20% of the invoice amount. Hotel porters get about C$1–2 per piece of luggage.

Peace Bridge in Calgary

WHEN TO GO

Apart from the coastal regions of British Columbia, Western Canada has an extreme climate with cold, snowy winters and dry, hot summers. The best time to travel (and high season) is mid June to late August. May and September are just as nice – with sunny days and cool nights. And in the autumn the vibrant colours of the forest foliage make a very beautiful display. February and March are best for snowmobiling and skiing in the Rockies.

ROAD ATLAS

The green line indicates the Discovery Tour 'Western Canada at a glance'
The blue line indicates the other Discovery Tours

All tours are also marked on the pull-out map

Photo: Mackenzie Delta

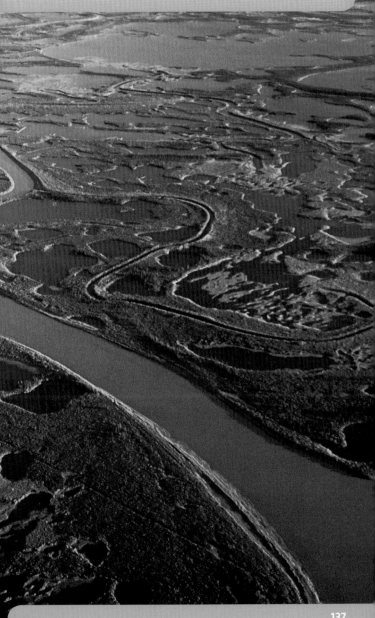

Exploring Western Canada

The map on the back cover shows how the area
has been sub-divided

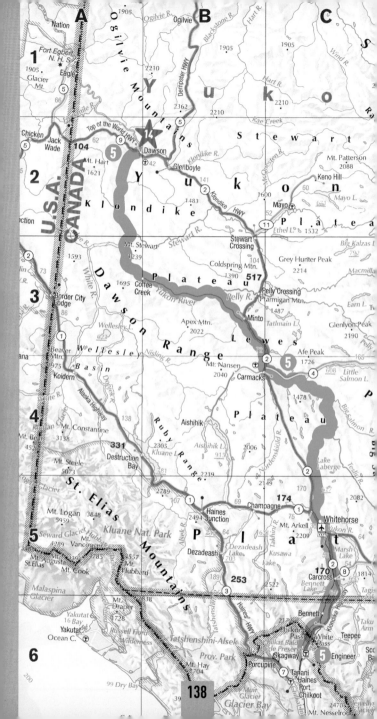

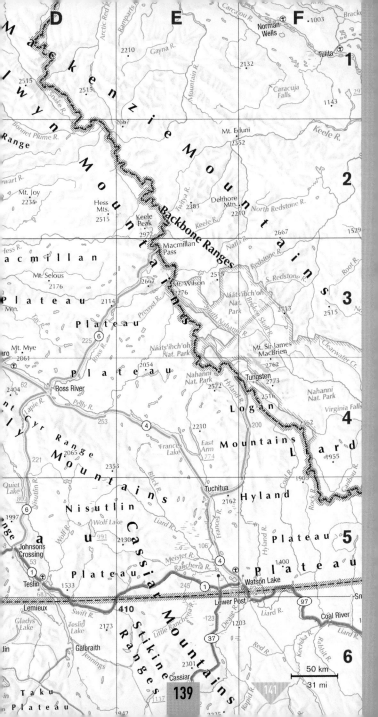

1

2

3

4

5

6

Mackenzie Mountains

Selwyn Range

Mackenzie Mountains

Backbone Ranges

Norman Wells

Tulita

•1003

•1143

Carcajou R.

Gayna R.

•2210

•2132

Caracuja Falls

Keele R.

Mt. Eduni
•2352

North Redstone R.

•2667

•1529

•2515

•2515

•2515

•2667

Snake R.

Bonnet Plume R.

Arctic Red R.

Wind R.

Bonnet Plume R.

Keele R.

Hart R.

Mt. Joy
•2235

Hess Mts.
•2515

Keele Peak
•2972

Macmillan Pass

Mt. Selous
•2176

•2114

Mt. Wilson
•2276

Mt. Mye
•2061

•2054

•2404

Ross River

•253

•2383

•2667

Delthore Mtn.
•2210

South Redstone R.

•2713

•2515

Náats'ihch'oh Nat. Park

South Nahanni R.

Náats'ihch'oh Nat. Park

•2515

Redstone R.

Root R.

Clearwater Cr.

Mt. Sir James MacBrien
•2762

Tungsten
•2773

•2516

Nahanni Nat. Park

Virginia Falls

Logan Mountains

•2572

Liard

•1955

Nahanni Nat. Park

•200

•362

Pelly R.

Lapie R.

Pelly R.

Frances Lake

East Arm
•774

•2210

•1903

Macmillan Plateau

Plateau

Plateau

Plateau

Mt.

•225

Ross R.

Prevost R.

Tay R.

•62

Pelly River

•221

•2065

•2353

Big R.

Black R.

Frances R.

Tuchitua

•2162

Hyland Plateau

Hyland R.

Coal R.

Caribou R.

Rock R.

Kechika R.

Rabbit R.

Liard R.

Liard R.

Hyland R.

•1400

•1533

•245

•106

Meister R.

Rancheria R.

Watson Lake

Lower Post

Liard R.

Coal River

Plateau

Plateau

Nisutlin

Nisutlin R.

Wolf R.

Wolf Lake

•991

•2130

Quiet Lake
•807

•1997

Johnsons Crossing

Teslin

Lemieux

•53

•683

Teslin Lake

•1533

Swift R.

•410

Little Rancheria R.

•123

•1203

Red R.

Rapid R.

Deese R.

•37

Gladys Lake

•2173

Galbraith

Jennings

•2301

Cassiar

•1117

Cassiar Mountains

Stikine Ranges

Taku Plateau

50 km

31 mi

139

141

•97

Sm

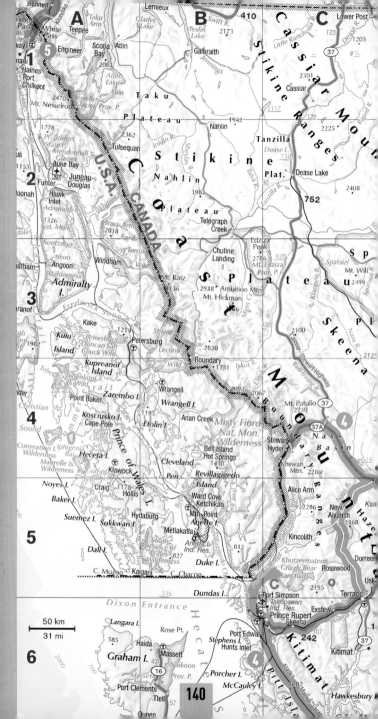

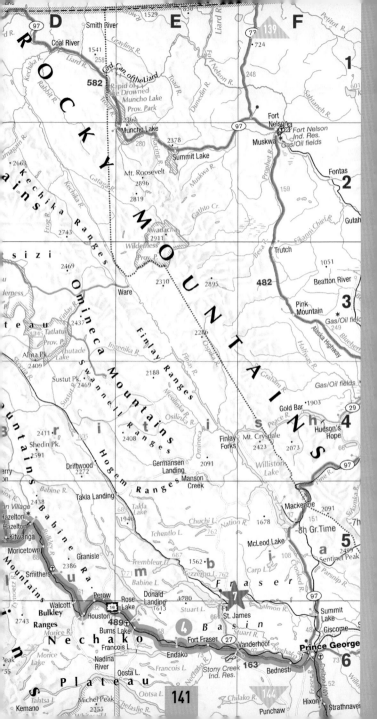

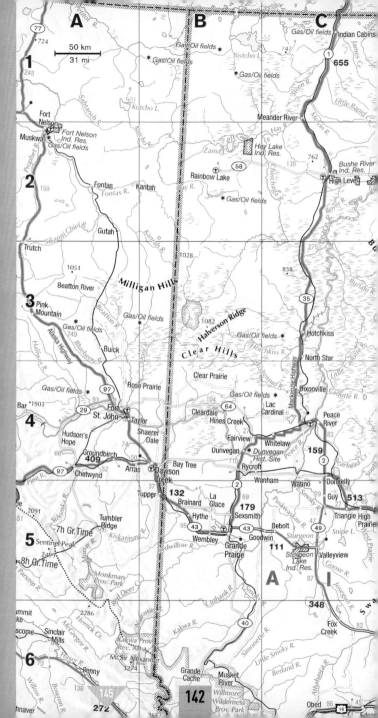

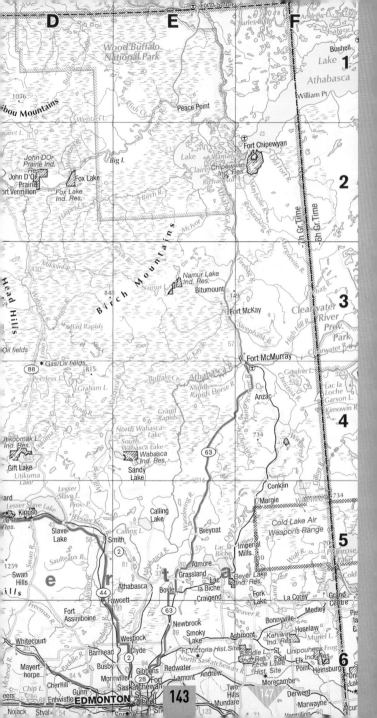

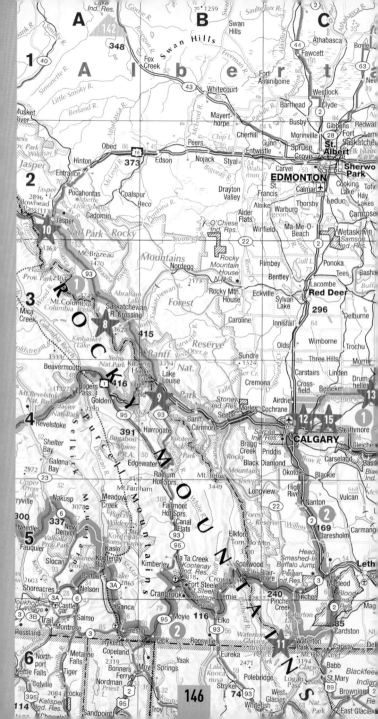

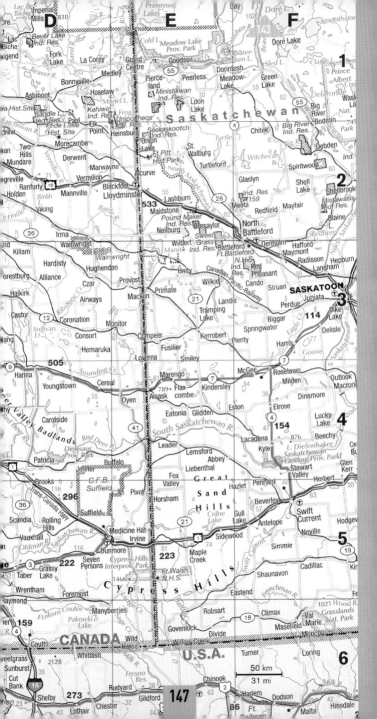

Top grid labels (left to right): D, E, F

Right-side grid labels (top to bottom): 1, 2, 3, 4, 5, 6

Lac La Biche
Imperial Mills
810
Wolf R.
Primrose Lake
Bay
Doré L.
Smoothston
143
Doré Lake
Bever Lake Ind. Res.
Fork Lake
La Corey
Grand Centre
Cold L.
Meadow Lake Prov. Park
Goodsoil
Waterhen L.
Sled L.
Beav
Clare
Prince Albert
Nat. Park
Bonnyville
Medley
55
Pierceland
Peerless
Dorintosh
Meadow Lake
Green Lake
82
55
Delaronde
Big River
Bodmin
747
Ashmont
Hoselaw
Muriel L.
Frog L.
Ministikwan Ind. Res.
Loon Lake
70
Saskatchewan
Big River Ind. Res.
4
Chitek
Debden
Ind.
Two Hills
Mundare
Morecambe
St. Paul Ind. Res.
Kehiwin Ind. Res.
Elk Point
Heinsburg
Frog L. Ind. Res.
Unipouheos Ind. Res.
Seekaskootch Ind. Res.
Onion Lake
Ft. Pitt Hist. Park
St. Walburg
Turtleford
Turtle L.
Witchekan L.
Spiritwood
80
Derwent
Marwayne
Acurve
North Saskatchewan R.
Glaslyn
Ind. Res.
159
Shell Lake
Shellbrook
Mistawasis Ind. Res.
Vegreville
Ranfurly
16
Vermilion
Blackfoot
Lloydminster
55
Lashburn
Maidstone
26
Meota
Redfield
Mayfair
Blaine
Holden
Viking
Birch L.
Mannville
533
Pound Maker Ind. Res.
Neilburg
Bresaylor
Sweet Grass Ind. Res.
Battle R.
North Battleford
Denholm
Hafford
Maymont
Redberry
36
Irma
Wainwright
C.F.B. Wainwright
Wilbert
Manito L.
63
Battleford
Ft. Battleford N.H.S. Ind. Res.
52
Radisson
Langham
Hepburn
Killam
Hardisty
Hughenden
Unity
Canadian-Pacific-Railway
Red Pheasant Ind. Res.
Cando
Struan
Perdue
SASKATOON
Forestburg
Alliance
Czar
Provost
Primate
Wilkie
Landis
Biggar
Juniata
114
3
Pike Lake
Halkirk
Airways
Macklin
Tramping Lake
Springwater
Harris
Delisle
Castor
12
Coronation
Monitor
Compeer
Kerrobert
Plenty
77
Goose
Sullivan L.
Consort
Hemaruka
Loverna
Smiley
Eagle Cr.
505
9
Hanna
Youngstown
Sounding Cr.
Cereal
Marengo
7
789
Flaxcombe
Alsask
McGee
Rosetown
84
Milden
Outlook
Macrorie
55
Oyen
Kindersley
Eston
Dinsmore
Carolside
Red Deer R.
Dinosaur Prov. Park
Badlands
41
South Saskatchewan R.
Eatonia
Glidden
Lacadena
Elrose
4
154
Lucky Lake
876
Beechy
L. Diefenbaker
Patricia
Brooks
Jenner
C.F.B. Suffield
Buffalo
Leader
Lemsford
Abbey
Liebenthal
Kyle
Saskatchewan Landing Prov. Park
Stewart Valley
Glen Kerr
Ce
54
Trans-Canada Hwy
116
296
Suffield
Pivot
Fox Valley
Horsham
Great Sand Hills
Hazlet
Pennant
Herbert
20
36
Scandia
Rolling Hills
Vauxhall
Medicine Hat
Irvine
Crane Lake
21
Gull Lake
Sidewood
Antelope
Beverley
57
Swift Current
63
Hodge
5
19
3
Grassy Lake
222
Seven Persons
Dunmore
Cypress Hills Interprov. Park
223
Maple Creek
Simmie
Neville
Cadillac
Taber
Wrentham
Foremost
Cypress Hills
Ft. Walsh N.H.S.
1466
Shaunavon
Eastend
Frenchman R.
1021 Wood R.
Grasslands Nat. Park
Etzikom Coulée
Manyberries
Pakowki Lake
Robsart
18
Govenlock
Divide
Climax
Val Marie
Masefield
Monch
159
4
Coutts
Whitlash
CANADA
Wild Horse
Willow Creek
U.S.A.
Turner
Loring
2128
Fresno Res.
50 km
31 mi
Milk R.
eetgrass
Sunburst
35
Cut Bank
15
Shelby
273
Rudyard
Gildford
147
Chinook
2
43
Harlem
Dodson
42
Hinsdale
Lothair
Chester
342
86
Ft.
Malta

Autobahn, mehrspurige Straße - in Bau Highway, multilane divided road - under construction		Autoroute, route à plusieurs voies - en construction Autopista, carretera de más carriles - en construcción
Fernverkehrsstraße - in Bau Trunk road - under construction		Route à grande circulation - en construction Ruta de larga distancia - en construcción
Hauptstraße Principal highway		Route principale Carretera principal
Nebenstraße Secondary road		Route secondaire Carretera secundaria
Fahrweg, Piste Practicable road, track		Chemin carrossable, piste Camino vecinal, pista
Straßennummerierung Road numbering	(1) 48 (1) (26) (26)	Numérotage des routes Numeración de carreteras
Entfernungen in mi. (USA), in km (CDN) Distances in mi. (USA), in km (CDN)	**259** 130 129	Distances en mi. (USA), en km (CDN) Distancias en mi. (USA), en km (CDN)
Höhe in Meter - Pass Height in meters - Pass	1365 •	Altitude en mètres - Col Altura en metros - Puerto de montaña
Eisenbahn Railway		Chemin-de-fer Ferrocarril
Autofähre - Schifffahrtslinie Car ferry - Shipping route		Bac autos - Ligne maritime Transportador de automóviles - Ferrocarriles
Wichtiger internationaler Flughafen - Flughafen Major international airport - Airport	✈ ✈	Aéroport important international - Aéroport Aeropuerto importante internacional - Aeropuerto
Internationale Grenze - Bundesstaatengrenze International boundary - federal boundary		Frontière nationale - Frontière fédérale Frontera nacional - Frontera federal
Unbestimmte Grenze Undefined boundary		Frontière d'État non définie Frontera indeterminada
Zeitzonengrenze Time zone boundary	-4h Greenwich Time -3h Greenwich Time	Limite de fuseau horaire Limite del huso horario
Hauptstadt eines souveränen Staates National capital	**OTTAWA**	Capitale nationale Capital de un estado soberano
Hauptstadt einer Provinz Provincial capital	**TORONTO**	Capitale d'un chef-lieu Capital de provincia
Sperrgebiet Restricted area		Zone interdite Zona prohibida
Indianerreservat - Nationalpark Indian reservation - National park		Réserve d'indiens - Parc national Reserva de indios - Parque nacional
Sehenswertes Kulturdenkmal Interesting cultural monument	★ Disneyland	Monument culturel intéressant Monumento cultural de interés
Sehenswertes Naturdenkmal Interesting natural monument	★ Niagara Falls	Monument naturel intéressant Monumento natural de interés
Brunnen, Salzsee Well, Salt lake		Puits, Lac salé Pozo, Lago salado
MARCO POLO Erlebnistour 1 MARCO POLO Discovery Tour 1		MARCO POLO Tour d'aventure 1 MARCO POLO Recorrido aventura 1
MARCO POLO Erlebnistouren MARCO POLO Discovery Tours		MARCO POLO Tours d'aventure MARCO POLO Recorridos de aventura
MARCO POLO Highlight	⭐1	MARCO POLO Highlight

MARCO POLO TRAVEL GUIDES

Algarve
Amsterdam
Andalucia
Athens
Australia
Austria
Bali & Lombok
Bangkok
Barcelona
Berlin
Brazil
Bruges
Brussels
Budapest
Bulgaria
California
Cambodia
Canada East
Canada West / Rockies
& Vancouver
Cape Town &
Garden Route
Cape Verde
Channel Islands
Chicago & The Lakes
China
Cologne
Copenhagen
Corfu
Costa Blanca
& Valencia
Costa Brava
Costa del Sol & Granada
Crete
Cuba
Cyprus (North and
South)
Devon & Cornwall
Dresden
Dubai
Dublin

Dubrovnik &
Dalmatian Coast
Edinburgh
Egypt
Egypt Red Sea Resorts
Finland
Florence
Florida
French Atlantic Coast
French Riviera
(Nice, Cannes & Monaco)
Fuerteventura
Gran Canaria
Greece
Hamburg
Hong Kong & Macau
Ibiza
Iceland
India
India South
Ireland
Israel
Istanbul
Italy
Japan
Jordan
Kos
Krakow
Lake District
Lake Garda
Lanzarote
Las Vegas
Lisbon
London
Los Angeles
Madeira & Porto Santo
Madrid
Mallorca
Malta & Gozo
Mauritius
Menorca

Milan
Montenegro
Morocco
Munich
Naples & Amalfi Coast
New York
New Zealand
Norway
Oslo
Oxford
Paris
Peru & Bolivia
Phuket
Portugal
Prague
Rhodes
Rome
Salzburg
San Francisco
Santorini
Sardinia
Scotland
Seychelles
Shanghai
Sicily
Singapore
South Africa
Sri Lanka
Stockholm
Switzerland
Tenerife
Thailand
Tokyo
Turkey
Turkey South Coast
Tuscany
United Arab Emirates
USA Southwest
(Las Vegas, Colorado,
New Mexico, Arizona
& Utah)
Venice
Vienna
Vietnam
Zakynthos & Ithaca,
Kefalonia, Lefkas

Travel with
Insider
Tips

INDEX

This index lists all sights and destinations featured in this guide.
Numbers in bold indicate a main entry.

CREDITS

WRITE TO US

e-mail: info@marcopologuides.co.uk
Did you have a great holiday?
Is there something on your mind?
Whatever it is, let us know!
Whether you want to praise, alert us
to errors or give us a personal tip –
MARCO POLO would be pleased to
hear from you.
We do everything we can to provide the
very latest information for your trip.

Nevertheless, despite all of our authors'
thorough research, errors can creep in.
MARCO POLO does not accept any
liability for this. Please contact us by
e-mail or post.
MARCO POLO Travel Publishing Ltd
Pinewood, Chineham Business Park
Crockford Lane, Chineham
Basingstoke, Hampshire RG24 8AL
United Kingdom

PICTURE CREDITS
Cover photograph: Emerald Lake in the Yoho National Park, Laif: Harscher
Photos: O. Bolch (20/21, 126/127); DuMont picture library: Hicker (flap left, flap right, 7, 10, 11, 17, 23, 24, 31, 42, 88, 124, 127); © fotolia.com: flucas (19 top); Getty Images/All Canada Photos: Wheatley (4 top); G. Hartmann (93); huber-images: P. Canali (12/1382/83), Damm (128 bottom), G. Simeone (62), M. Verin (2); Kitewing Sports Ltd.: Justin Bufton (18 centre); Lade-Okapia: Don (126); Laif: Harscher (1), Laif: Heeb (4 bottom, 52), Hub (9); Laif/hemis.fr (8); H. Lange (125); mauritius images/age (36, 68, 121); mauritius images/Alamy (26/27, 28 left, 28 right, 29, 58/59, 65, 66/67, 71, 75, 78, 84, 87, 90, 101, 102/103, 108, 114, 118/119, 122/123, 135, 140/141), M. Bruxelle (32/33), M. P. O'Neill (45), B. Stanley (19 bottom); mauritius images/Alamy/All Canada Photos (6, 46/47); mauritius images/Alaska Stock: K. Smith (54); mauritius images/Aurora Photos (61); mauritius images/Axiom Photographic (14/15); mauritius images/Firstlight (40/41); mauritius images/Imagebroker: N. Eisele-Hein (76), J. Pfatschbacher (72/73), E. Strigl (96, 129), S. Wackerhagen (94/95, 99, 116); mauritius images/SuperStock (48); mauritius images/Travel Collection (34, 39); mauritius images/Westend61/Fotofeeling (50/51); T. Stankiewicz (30, 81, 128 top); K. Teuschl (5, 18 bottom, 111); VAN DOP GALLERY: Trudy Van Dop (18 top)

3rd edition 2019
fully revised and updated
Worldwide Distribution: Marco Polo Travel Publishing Ltd, Pinewood, Chineham Business Park, Crockford Lane, Basingstoke, Hampshire RG24 8AL, United Kingdom. E-mail: sales@marcopolouk.com
© MAIRDUMONT GmbH & Co. KG, Ostfildern
Chief editor: Marion Zorn
Author: Karl Teuschl; editor: Marlis v. Hessert-Fraatz
Programme supervision: Lucas Forst-Gill, Susanne Heimburger, Tamara Hub, Johanna Jiranek, Nikolai Michaelis, Kristin Wittemann, Tim Wohlbold
Picture editor: Gabriele Forst
Cartography road atlas & pull-out map: © MAIRDUMONT, Ostfildern
Cover design, p. 1, pull-out map cover: Karl Anders – Büro für Brand Profiling, Hamburg; design inside: milchhof:atelier, Berlin; design p. 2/3, Discovery Tours: Susan Chaaban Dipl.-Des. (FH)
Translated from German by Wendy Barrow, Rupert Kindermann and Lindsay Chalmers-Gerbracht
Editorial office: SAW Communications, Redaktionsbüro Dr. Sabine A. Werner, Mainz: Frauke Feuchter, Julia Gilcher, Dr. Sabine A. Werner; prepress: SAW Communications, Mainz, in cooperation with alles mit Medien, Mainz

DOS & DON'TS ✋

A few things you should bear in mind on your holiday

DO TRAVEL WITH HEALTH INSURANCE

As a foreigner you will be treated as a private patient and a day at a Canadian clinic can easily cost C$1000 and more. Ensure that you have foreign health insurance.

DO SCARE OFF THE BEARS

Bears have an excellent sense of smell but have poor eyesight. If you are out walking upwind and surprise a bear they will be aggressive. When hiking it is best to talk loudly, sing or wear a bell on your leg so that you announce yourself and give any bears in the area time to move away.

DON'T UNDERESTIMATE DISTANCES

Canada is a massive country and distances on the map can be deceiving. Especially in the vast north of the country where the width of a finger on the map can mean a very long day trip on seemingly endless dirt roads.

DON'T GIVE THIEVES AN OPPORTUNITY

Canada is a very safe destination; however, it is always best not to give thieves an opportunity. So never leave cameras or other valuables in the car and at night avoid dark streets in the large cities.

DON'T DRIVE UNDER THE INFLUENCE OF ALCOHOL

Although the limit is 0.8, in the event of an accident the insurance company will not pay out. In addition, the police show no mercy and the penalties are draconian.

DO BE AWARE OF THE SMOKING LAWS

Smoking is frowned upon in Canada – and it is horrendously expensive. Smoking is prohibited in all public buildings, airports, and restaurants. Only in the furthest corner you might still find a smoking section.

DO INFORM AUTHORITIES BEFORE SETTING OFF ON A HIKE

Whether it is just for a day, a week or an entire month that you plan for a hike or canoe trip: always leave a note with your hiking or canoeing route and the time of your return. Leave the information with canoe rentals, the bush pilots that take you into the hinterland, or with the wardens in the national parks.

All police stations (RCMP) will also accept these notes. If indeed something does go wrong, a search party can be sent out immediately. Please do not forget to report back once you have returned safely.